CHILDREN OF THE PROMISE

FAITH-BUILDING STORIES

FOR KIDS

SO- BTS - 937

D1712183

Also by Cari J. Haus:
Faith-building Stories for Kids:

A Brand-new World: Adam and Eve
God Makes a Promise: Noah
Father of Many Nations: Abraham
Learning to Walk With God, with Dwight Hall

To order, call 1-800-765-6955.

Visit us at
www.AutumnHousePublishing.com
for information on other Autumn House® products.

CHILDREN OF THE PROMISE
FAITH-BUILDING STORIES
FOR KIDS

Autumn
House® Publishing
www.autumnhousepublishing.com
A Division of REVIEW AND HERALD® PUBLISHING
Since 1861

Copyright © 2007 by Review and Herald® Publishing Association

Published by Autumn House® Publishing, a division of Review and Herald® Publishing, Hagerstown, MD 21741-1119

All rights reserved. No portion of this book may be reproduced, stored in a retrieval system, or transmitted in any form or by any means (electronic, mechanical, photocopy, recording, scanning, or other), except for brief quotations in critical reviews or articles, without the prior written permission of the publisher.

Autumn House® titles may be purchased in bulk for educational, business, fund-raising, or sales promotional use. For information, please e-mail SpecialMarkets@reviewandherald.com.

Autumn House® Publishing publishes biblically based materials for spiritual, physical, and mental growth and Christian discipleship.

The author assumes full responsibility for the accuracy of all facts and quotations as cited in this book.

Unless otherwise noted, texts are from the *Holy Bible, New International Version.* Copyright © 1973, 1978, 1984, International Bible Society. Used by permission of Zondervan Bible Publishers.

Bible texts credited to Amplified are from *The Amplified Bible,* Old Testament copyright © 1965, 1987 by the Zondervan Corporation. The *Amplified New Testament* copyright © 1958, 1987 by The Lockman Foundation. Used by permission.

Texts credited to NKJV are from the New King James Version. Copyright © 1979, 1980, 1982 by Thomas Nelson, Inc. Used by permission. All rights reserved.

This book was
Edited by Penny Estes Wheeler
Cover design by Ron Pride
Cover art by Jo Card
Typeset: 11/13 Cheltenham

PRINTED IN U.S.A.

11 10 09   08 07   5 4 3 2 1

Library of Congress Cataloging-in-Publication Data
Haus, Cari Hoyt.
  Children of the Promise : faith-building stories for kids / Cari Haus.
       p. cm. — (Faith-building stories for kids)
    ISBN 978-0-8127-0439-6
  1. Jacob (Biblical patriarch)—Juvenile literature.   2. Esau (Biblical figure)—Juvenile literature.   3. Joseph (Biblical patriarch)—Juvenile literature.   4. Bible stories, English.—O.T. Genesis.   I. Title.
  BS580.J3H38 2007
  222'.1109505—dc22

                                                      2006035711

Contents

CHAPTER 1

Waiting for a Baby

The first few years of marriage should be one of the sweetest times in life. There are so many things to find out about each other, talk about, and do. This was especially true with Isaac and Rebekah. Since they'd never met each other before their wedding day, they had lots of things to find out.

"What's your favorite color?"

"Which would you like for me to pick for you—roses, poppies, or lilies?"

"Do you like onions? Do you like dates and almonds? What about melons?"

The list of questions—and surprises—that Isaac and Rebekah had for each other must have gone on for months, if not years. And just like others of their time who expected their home to be filled with children, I'm sure they asked the same question that couples discuss even today.

"Do you like children?" Isaac asked Rebekah.

"I love them," she replied with shining eyes. "I can hardly wait until we have a few of our own."

"Good thing!" A smile played around the corners of Isaac's mouth. "In case you haven't heard, I'm supposed to be the father of many nations. And that prediction, my dear, must involve you, too."

"Oh!" Rebekah must have gasped. "I guess I will be pretty busy."

Perhaps Isaac and Rebekah hoped their first baby would come a year or two after their marriage. But before they knew it, two years had gone by. Then three, and four, and five! They had everything they wanted except children.

After just a couple of years Isaac and Rebekah feared that they had the same trouble that was such a trial to Abraham and Sarah—that they were unable to have children. This might not seem like a big deal to couples who don't care whether they have children, but it was a very big deal to Isaac and Rebekah.

It's easy to hear the unbelievers snickering behind Isaac's back.

"He's supposed to be the father of many nations, but he's off to a slow start. Give him time, though. His dad was nearly 100 when Isaac came along. Isaac here is only 50."

This was hard for Rebekah, too, for she longed for children to make their home complete. The Bible tells us that Isaac was 40 years old when he married

Rebekah, and 60 years old when she finally had a child. That means that Isaac and Rebekah waited 20 long years for a baby.

To Isaac's credit, he didn't make the mistake that his father had made, and marry a second wife. His own childhood had been marred by Ishmael's bitter taunts, and Isaac wasn't about to bring that into his home. Then again, God had promised to make him the father of many nations. God had also hand-picked his wife. That pretty much settled it for Isaac. He knew that God could take care of the rest.

But that didn't keep him from praying about it. The Bible tells us that he prayed to the Lord about giving Rebekah a baby, and God answered that prayer with a yes.

Rebekah had never been happier. "At long last, we're going to have our very own baby!" she told Isaac as she grabbed his hands and spun around. At last she could use the little gowns she'd sewn so long before. At last she could sit with the other mothers and watch her children play. But as the months went by a worried little frown often touched her face. Something was just a little strange about this baby.

For a tiny baby, this one surely kicks in all directions, she thought. Rebekah didn't know it yet, but the tussling would continue for many years to come. For as an angel soon told her, there was not one but two baby boys in her belly. And they started their struggle at a very young age, with their first wrestling match before they were born. Unfortunately, it was the first of many more to come.

CHAPTER 2

Jacob and Esau—
Tussling Twins

Imagine if you won the lottery on the day you were born. Imagine if, from the moment you opened your eyes at birth, you were destined to be rich, very rich. Imagine if, in addition to having fistfuls of money in your pocket every step of life's way, you were also born to be the leader of your very wealthy parents' entire household. And imagine if all of this was yours simply because you were your parents' *first* son.

That is what the birthright is all about. A birthright doesn't mean much in our culture, but it meant a great deal in the days of Jacob and Esau. One son got it; one didn't. One would be the leader; one wouldn't. One

11

would get a double portion of everything his father owned; one would not. In the case of twin boys such as these, it was all determined by who was born first. With this in mind, it seems fitting that the tussle in Rebekah's belly got so wild that she went to "inquire of the Lord."

If babies Jacob and Esau had known about the birthright, their before-birth wrestling match might have been even worse. As it was, their series of somersaults definitely got their mother's attention and most likely the attention of Isaac.

"I bet that's an elbow!"

"That feels like a foot!"

"Hey! That felt like *three* feet! What's happening in there?"

You have to remember that twins weren't very common when these twins were born. So though Rebekah was thrilled that she was finally going to have a baby, she expected only one. It must have been quite a shock when the angel told her that two babies were on the way. Even more shocking, the angel said that the older would serve the younger. This went against the birthright customs of those days when the firstborn was always the leader.

Since Jacob and Esau were twins, you can be sure that Jacob didn't miss being first by much. The Bible, which is silent on many things, gives an amazing little detail about the birth of Jacob and Esau. It says that when they were born, Jacob's little hand had a grip on Esau's heel.

It's as if he was saying, "You might have gotten out first, but you know what the angel said. The birthright belongs to me."

Now, twins that look just alike are called identical

twins, and those are the ones we usually notice. But these twins looked nothing alike! It's hard to imagine a baby that is already hairy, but that's what the Bible says about Esau. He was ruddy, or rosy-skinned, and hairy. Jacob, the younger of the two, was smooth-skinned and nothing like his older brother.

As the boys grew up, the difference between them became more and more pronounced. Esau was a bit of a daredevil and a very good hunter. Jacob was a quiet homebody, content to watch the sheep and help his mother with her duties. Esau was selfish and lived for the moment, while Jacob cared about others and was always thinking ahead.

Esau was not much interested in spiritual things. In fact, the New International Version of the Bible calls him godless (see Hebrews 12:16), while the King James Version calls him profane.

But Jacob loved God and wanted to serve Him with all his heart. He especially wanted the birthright because it would make him the family's spiritual leader.

Isaac, who was a quiet man, liked to hear Esau's stories of his daring exploits. He also loved the rich, flavorful venison from the deer Esau hunted and killed. Rebekah, however, was much more impressed with the helpfulness and spiritual nature of Jacob. And so Isaac and Rebekah made the mistake that parents should never make. They each had a favorite child.

It's amazing how one big mistake can upset what should have been a very peaceful life. In many ways Rebekah was an excellent mother. She spent hours teaching her children about Jesus and the promise God gave to Abraham. She tried to teach them to be courteous, helpful, and thoughtful—just as she was. It must have been very frustrating to her when Esau shut his ears to spiritual things. But she should not have favored Jacob over Esau. The Bible tells us that "God is no respecter of persons" (Acts 10:34, KJV). That means He loves all people the same. God is fair. Even when we make bad choices, He does not play favorites. And Rebekah shouldn't have either.

Unfortunately, Isaac struggled with the exact same problem. He was so fascinated with Esau's adventures and so close to his firstborn son that he was almost blinded to the fact that Esau had drifted further and further away from God.

CHAPTER 3

The Most Expensive Lentils in the World

"If I don't get food soon, I think I'll just die!" Every fiber in Esau's body cried out for food as he stumbled toward camp. After a long and unsuccessful day of hunting, he had only one thing on his mind. He'd give anything for a big bite of something good—and he wanted it now! If there had been a fast-food restaurant nearby he would have barged right in and ordered every item on the menu. But there was no place around where he could get a meal in a minute. The closest cook, as it turned out, was his brother. And Jacob wasn't exactly in a mood to give him anything.

It seems that things had been building up to this moment for quite some time. Although Esau had the birthright, he couldn't have cared less about it. In fact, the spiritual side of the birthright seemed like a burden to him. On the other hand, Jacob desperately wanted the birthright. But now the tables were turned. For once in his life Jacob had something Esau just had to have, and as far as Jacob was concerned it was time for a trade.

You see, more than anything else in the world Jacob wanted the birthright, and it wasn't the money he wanted. Jacob was fascinated by the stories of how God had talked with Abraham and how God Himself had chosen Isaac's wife. The spiritual blessing that went with the birthright was what he longed for with all his heart. The thought of somehow wriggling it away from Esau was never out of his mind.

As for Esau, he really didn't care. His main goal in life was to do as he pleased. If Esau were alive today, he might be known as a party animal. He loved power, riches, and a wild, roving life.

Jacob loved God and wanted to do what was right, but he hadn't fully given his heart to Him. Like his mother, he still didn't truly trust God. He should have known that since the Lord had said the birthright would be his, God would make it happen. Instead, Jacob was always thinking up new ways to steal it from Esau.

Now is my chance, Jacob thought when he saw how famished Esau was. The closest thing to fast food nearby happened to be a pot of lentils cooked by none other than Jacob himself.

Esau, who wasn't much of a negotiator, got right to the point.

"Give me a bowl of lentils," he bellowed, "or I'm going to die!"

Jacob had been waiting for this moment, this delicious opportunity, when he would have Esau right where he wanted him.

"Not so fast, brother." Jacob stepped between Esau and the rich, thick, wonderfully seasoned soup. There was a price to be paid for these lentils.

Jacob spelled out the deal. "Sell me your birthright, and I'll give you some soup."

"OK. Fine! I'm about to die of hunger. What good is the birthright to me?"

But Jacob didn't give it to him yet. He wanted a receipt for the sale in the form of a very solemn promise. You know that when people go to testify before a judge, they hold up their right hand and take an oath to tell the truth. Well, this is what Jacob made Esau do—right over the pot of lentils. He made Esau swear that he was giving up all rights to his birthright. True to his careful nature, Jacob left nothing to chance.

At this point in his life Esau felt relieved at the idea of getting rid of the birthright. The person who had it was to be the spiritual leader, or priest, of the home. He also must marry someone who loved and honored God.

Isaac had patiently waited for Abraham to find the right wife for him, but Esau was not the patient sort. He had gone out and picked himself not one but two wives from the pagan families who lived nearby. The Bible tells us that the wives of Esau caused real grief to Isaac and Rebekah. No doubt things became even worse as grandchildren came into the picture.

More than anything else, Isaac and Rebekah wanted to tell those children about the God of heaven and teach them to love Him as they did. But Esau was more interested in teaching his sons to hunt than in telling them about the true God. And Esau's wives were raising his children in the way they had been raised, teaching them to bow down to idols of wood and clay. What a sad thing for Isaac and Rebekah to have to watch in what should have been their happy golden years.

So Esau sold his birthright to Jacob for a bowl of lentils and felt glad about it too. Meanwhile, the home of Isaac and Rebekah, which had been so happy for so many years, came closer and closer to a pile of trouble that would haunt them the rest of their lives.

CHAPTER 4

Getting Ahead
of God

Have you ever heard the old saying "The end doesn't justify the means"?

What this is trying to tell us is that it is never right to do wrong, even if doing that wrong would bring about something good. It was a lesson that Jacob and Rebekah had to learn the hard way, and they paid a very bitter price for their sin.

A number of years had come and gone since Esau had thoughtlessly sold his birthright to Jacob for a bowl of lentils. Despite the solemn pledge Esau had made, Jacob still worried about the birthright quite a bit. It was as if Jacob was looking for a bag of gold and—

until he had it firmly in his grasp—was afraid it would slip away.

What if Esau goes back on his promise? Jacob wondered. Esau wasn't exactly a moral man, so Jacob had plenty of reason to worry. Rebekah worried about the birthright too. Although she is often remembered for the one great mistake of her life, she was a godly woman. She loved the one true God and understood that Jacob was the son best suited to raise children who would be a light in the world and an honor to Him.

You can be sure that Jacob had told Isaac that Esau had sold the birthright for a bowl of lentils. And, of course, Isaac knew that an angel from God had told Rebekah that the younger boy would rule the older. He knew, too, that Jacob and Rebekah didn't want the birthright to go to Esau, and that Esau didn't care one whit about having it. Yet somehow, deep down in his heart, Isaac badly wanted to give the birthright to his older son.

Isaac was a peaceful man, and the last thing he wanted was a family feud. He was elderly now, and going blind, but his mind was still pretty sharp. As he thought about the matter, Isaac decided the best way to accomplish what he wanted was to give Esau the birthright in secret.

It was the custom to have a big feast on such special occasions, but Isaac had a plan for that, too. Esau was a terrific game hunter, and Isaac loved to dine on the meat his son killed and cooked.

"Go hunting, and bring back some meat," Isaac whispered to Esau. "Make me some of your wonderful venison. After we have a special meal together I will give you the birthright blessing. I may die soon, and that way you will be sure to have it before I go."

While Esau couldn't have cared less about the spiritual blessing of the birthright—and was even glad to be rid of it—he did understand that the son who received the birthright would get twice as much as the other when his father died. That meant if Isaac had 30,000 shekels, which were like the dollars of those days, one son would get 20,000 and one son would get 10,000. And it went like that in the dividing of everything Isaac had. The son with the birthright would get twice as much as any other son.

Esau was not a mathematical genius, but he had this one figured out. He liked money, and he liked to spend it. It seems safe to say that, in spite of his wayward life, Esau also loved his father very much. Isaac had been good to him, and Esau wanted to please him. So he got out his bow and arrows and went on a quick hunting trip.

Have you ever been around someone—maybe your mother or grandma—who could hear your hand in the cookie jar from virtually any room in the house? Did you ever try to sneak just one cookie— and end up getting caught with your hand in the jar?

Rebekah must have had ears like this. She knew Isaac very well. She knew what he wanted. And she knew what was going on in her house.

The whole rest of this story could have been avoided if Isaac and Rebekah had taken the matter up with God. No doubt God would have been happy to send his angel to remind Isaac of whom the birthright should go to. He could also have impressed Rebekah that letting God take care of the situation was how she could show her faith. But this didn't happen, because Isaac and Rebekah didn't ask. Isaac had his secret plan in motion, and Rebekah had hers.

"Come here quickly," she whispered to Jacob. "Your father is planning to give Esau the birthright today!"

Jacob's face turned pale. All his hopes and plans were about to go down the drain. The thing he valued the most was about to be given to the person who valued it the least. If he didn't shed a few tears, he must have wanted to very badly. But this was no time to sit around feeling sorry. Rebekah had a plan.

It was a daring plan—a "risk everything" idea that could result in a curse if it backfired.

Rebekah wanted Jacob to dress up like Esau and take a wonderful meal to his father. He was to trick Isaac into giving him the birthright!

Jacob was shocked at the very idea. As badly as he wanted the birthright, he knew that telling a lie was wrong.

"Don't worry about being caught," Rebekah told him, using all her power of persuasion to encourage Jacob to do it. "Can you imagine what will happen to God's plan if Esau gets the birthright? He doesn't even love God and couldn't care less about the birthright."

"But what if Father figures out who I am?" Jacob asked. After all, it wasn't as if he had had much practice in lying, and this was a pretty tricky deception. "Esau is hairy; I'm not. Esau smells like the field, and I don't. He even talks different from me."

Rebekah had an answer for everything. Isaac must have been very blind and Esau very hairy, because she had Jacob put animal skins on his neck and hands to make him feel more like Esau. The skins would make Jacob smell more like the field too, and as for the voice—well, he would just have to fake it.

So the stage was set for trickery in a family that knew better. And the family feud that Isaac was trying to avoid was about to get started.

CHAPTER 5

"Bless Me, My Father"

Jacob's hands trembled, and his knees knocked together as he stepped into the room of the large tent where Isaac was waiting for Esau. Once he was in, there was no going back. So he took a deep breath, squared his shoulders, and acted just like his brother.

For some reason, Isaac was quite suspicious.

"Come over here, so I can feel you," he said. He even went so far as to say, "The voice is the voice of Jacob, but the hands are the hands of Esau."

Rebekah must have been holding her breath in the background while somehow Jacob carried it off. Father and younger son had a fine meal together, although Jacob must have enjoyed it much less than did Isaac.

What will happen if Esau walks in right now? he thought desperately, chewing the meat that his mother had prepared. It was hard to swallow when the food went down to the sinking feeling in the pit of his stomach. But at last Isaac gave Jacob the blessing he had wanted so badly and waited for so long. Sadly, he couldn't enjoy the words as he should have. All he could think of was getting away. He wanted to escape—from the deception and the lying words that fell from his lips—as quickly as possible.

As things turned out, Jacob had a close call. Just as he was walking out one side of Isaac's tent, Esau came in the other. No doubt Rebekah sent Jacob out to the field in a hurry. Then she stood by to see what would happen next.

She didn't have long to wait.

Esau strode in with a platter of delicious-smelling steak. "Here is the venison I made for you," he said happily.

"Who are you?" Isaac demanded in a loud, quivering voice.

"I am your son, your firstborn!"

Isaac was shocked. A terrible lie had just taken place in his home. He was deeply disappointed in Jacob and horrified at the sadness Esau would soon feel.

"Your brother was already here," he groaned. "I gave him the blessing, and he will be blessed."

It's amazing how, when something we never cared about is gone forever, it somehow becomes very valuable to us. For years Esau had wanted to lose the birthright. But now, when it was gone forever, he wanted it back very badly.

Isaac knew that his giving Jacob the birthright would hurt Esau, but he was not ready for the outpouring of grief from his older son. Esau was crushed. He was angry. He was weeping and shaking and yelling all in one furious fit.

This was one part of the plan that Rebekah hadn't worked out. She had probably thought that since Esau didn't care about the birthright anyway, he would just get over it. But Esau did not get over it. He told all of his friends, in no uncertain terms, exactly what he would do to his brother once their father died. And it wasn't a pretty thought.

Rebekah, who always seemed to have her ear to the ground, got the picture. Jacob—the son she loved so dearly, the one who'd listened to what she had taught him about God and who was always gentle and kind to her—faced death at the hands of his own brother. Rebekah could have trusted God to keep this from happening, but she didn't. Somehow it seemed easier to swing into action again. And again she had a plan. And she went right to Isaac.

"I am so tired of my daughters-in-law," she complained, talking about Esau's two wives. "They are wearing me out with their heathen ways. If Jacob marries someone like that, my heart will break. Why don't we send him back to my brother and family to find a wife there—a nice girl who loves and honors God?"

This time Isaac agreed. He knew only too well how angry Esau was, and perhaps he too feared for Jacob's life. In his heart he also knew that God had promised the birthright to Jacob and that he should not have tried to give it to Esau.

Sad to say, Rebekah, the girl whose love story had started so wonderfully so many years before, paid a very high price for the whole sad affair. Esau was enraged at his mother for her part in Jacob's lie, and Jacob, the son who truly loved and cared for her, now packed up a few things and ran for his life.

There was no going-away party for Jacob. There was no brightly decorated camel caravan loaded to take him to look for a wife, and no rich gifts to give her. There was only a secret goodbye, and a very sad one at that. Jacob and Rebekah may have tried to be cheerful. Maybe they said that they would see each other again. But in their hearts they feared that this goodbye was forever.

We can imagine Jacob giving his mother one last kiss, and then another. We can imagine Rebekah shading her eyes and watching until Jacob was only a dark speck in the distance. We can imagine her going back to her tent and crying as though her heart would break. She had no one to blame but herself, and that is the saddest grief of all.

They didn't know it then, but their worst fears were going to come true. Jacob, who left home with a bundle of guilt weighing down his shoulders, would never see his mother in this world again.

CHAPTER 6

A Rock for a Pillow

Taking a trip—especially to a faraway place—is usually a lot of fun. You have the excitement of seeing new people, places, and cultures. You experience new sights and sounds, such as viewing the scenery rushing by from a train as it thunders down the tracks, or looking down at the ocean from a jet as it roars into the sky.

But Jacob felt none of these happy things as he began his trip to his mother's homeland. To begin with, he had to walk. There was no such thing as scenery "rushing by." In fact, "crawling" would be a better word to describe it. He put one foot in front of the other until at last he looked back to see the tents as just a smudge against the sky. The whole empty world lay ahead of him, and he walked on, following a path of guilt.

Then there was the fear that plagued him every step of the way. You see, Jacob was running from Esau, and there were good reasons to be afraid of his brother.

Esau was very angry, as well as a very good hunter, and he had a lot of friends in the nearby tribes who would be glad to help track his brother down. So here was Jacob, the son of one of the richest men in his world, but he sure didn't look like it. When Eliezer had gone to find a wife for Isaac, a caravan of camels and a number of servants had traveled with him, not to mention the gold and silver he carried as gifts.

Jacob probably had all the money he could carry in a small bag that hung from his belt—just a few pieces of silver. Other than that, he had the clothes on his back and a wooden walking stick known in those days as a staff. That was it.

To make matters worse, Jacob was almost afraid to pray. Here he was—a man who loved his home and family—leaving home for good. It was the darkest hour of his life, a time when he needed God more than anything else in the world. Yet he felt so bad about his sin of lying to his father that he wondered whether God would still have him.

Many years later the book of Proverbs pointed out that lying is one of the seven sins God particularly hates. Of course, that wasn't written in Jacob's day, yet he knew that lying was very wrong. He knew that God is great and pure and good. And he felt so horrible about the lie he'd told his father that he hardly dared to ask God for forgiveness. He was afraid that God wouldn't forgive him.

Sometimes our minds get mixed up. Sometimes when we get to thinking one way, it's hard to turn things around. When we get really sad or discouraged or afraid God has different ways of trying to help us pop out of it. Sometimes He sends a cheerful person to us with just the right words to make us feel better. Sometimes we might see a beautiful flower or pretty bird. Or a playful puppy might brighten a very dark day.

It would have been good for Jacob to have someone to talk to, but he was very much alone. He didn't have a cell phone to touch base with his mom. He didn't have an MP3 player to drown out the sad thoughts that kept running through his mind. And when night came and he stopped to rest, he didn't even have a pillow to put his head on.

This is why, by the second night of his journey, he was very discouraged. He was afraid for his life. He was far from his family and friends. The night was chilly, and he didn't have a sleeping bag. He lay on the ground and put a rock under his head for a pillow. But it was here—when Jacob was flat on his back—that he finally decided to look up to God. Perhaps the stars twinkling down over his head reminded him of God's promise to Abraham, the promise that he would have so many children that they would be like the millions and millions of stars.

Before Jacob had left home, Isaac had given him the promised blessing one more time. Yet Jacob felt he had let God down so badly that the blessing could

not truly be his. But though Jacob felt very far from God, God was not far from him. God had not left Jacob. He was simply waiting for Jacob to get far enough down that he had to look up.

So that night, alone and lonely, Jacob prayed as he'd never prayed before. He was a grown man, but he cried like a baby. He told God how very sorry he was for what he had done. He asked God to still give him the blessing. He asked for forgiveness and promised that with God's help he would be a much better man.

When Jacob was too tired to cry anymore, he lay his head on the hard, cold pillow and fell fast asleep. And there, under the starry skies that held such a message of promise for Jacob, God sent him a dream. In Jacob's dream he saw beautiful steps going right from his rocky pillow all the way up to heaven. He saw angels with happy faces and white robes and wings walking up and down the towering staircase. And right there, when all his friends and family were far away, God came very close to Jacob.

"I am the Lord God of Abraham your father, and of Isaac," a voice boomed from the heavens. "I will be with you and bless you." Jacob could hardly believe his ears, but God had more to tell him. "All families of the earth will be blessed because of you, and I will give you this land."

When God made this promise, He was telling Jacob that Jesus would be one of his great-great- and very great grandchildren. In fact, Jacob's whole dream was really about Jesus, who would one day come as the Messiah.

The steps in Jacob's dream were a symbol to

show Jacob something very important about God. Sin had made a terrible separation between heaven and earth. In heaven everything is right and beautiful and good, but on earth there are selfishness, hatred, and evil. But when God the Son came to earth as a baby named Jesus, He came to be a bridge between heaven and earth. By coming here as a baby, He brought heaven very near to—and even right down to—this earth. And because of that bridge, God's angels can go back and forth, bringing comfort and help to the poor wayward people down here.

Comfort and help were what Jacob needed during this very dark hour of his life, and God made sure that he got them.

When Jacob awoke from his dream, he felt the warmth of God's wonderful presence around him. His stony pillow didn't seem cold anymore.

"Surely the Lord is in this place," Jacob said to himself, "and I knew it not. . . . This is none other but the house of God, and this is the gate of heaven" (Genesis 28:16, 17, KJV).

At first morning light Jacob took the stone he had slept on and stood it up like a pillar. Then he held a special little ceremony to celebrate just how special this place, which he named Bethel, really was.

Gone were his tears from the night before. Gone were his fear and sadness. Jacob now knew for sure that even though he had sinned and dishonored God by his lies, God was still by his side. God loved him! God had forgiven him!

Right then and there Jacob made a promise—a promise he kept for the rest of his life. He didn't know what the road ahead would bring, but he knew that he,

Jacob, would serve and honor God. He told God that if He would be with him as He had promised, he would be faithful in everything he did. He even promised God that he would pay tithe.

What a beautiful ending to an otherwise very sad story. Jacob still missed his parents. There was still a price to pay for his sin. He was still on a dangerous journey. But he had this assurance: God would be by his side.

This is a promise that you can claim as well. Whether you walk through a flowery meadow or a cloud-covered valley, God will be by your side. He loves you just as much as He loved Jacob! You are not alone. He will not leave you. So look up! Look up at the stars and think about God's love to you. Look into the sky and think about how, very soon, Jesus will come and fill the sky with clouds of glory. If you feel that you have no friends or if your family is mad at you or far away, God will be there for you. He will put His arms of love around you just as He did for Jacob if you let Him. Why not start looking up today?

CHAPTER • 7

Man at the
Well—Again

After his dream at Bethel Jacob continued his trip toward the land of his mother's family. But now he walked with a happy heart, with a sureness and confidence that were missing before. For now he had the assurance that God was with him, that God would be there for him just as He had been for his father, Isaac, and his grandfather Abraham.

It's amazing how history repeats itself in little ways, yet in other ways is so different. Many years had gone by since Abraham's servant Eliezer had met Rebekah at the well. Eliezer's caravan had been truly impressive—complete with 10 camels, numerous servants, and lots of rich gifts for the future wife of Isaac.

And now, many years later, a stranger waited at the well again. Only this one didn't have a camel, servants, or money. He had little more than the clothes on his back, and, given the length of his journey, they were dusty, tattered, and ragged.

This man was looking for a wife too, but he would have to get one the hard way. He would have to earn the right to marry the bride of his choice. You see, the people had a few customs in those days that we could learn from today. Fathers wouldn't dream of letting their daughter marry a man until he showed that he could provide for a wife and children. In order to prove this, the would-be husband had to give the father of the bride a gift that was known as a dowry.

Giving a dowry for Rebekah had been no problem for someone like Isaac, who was the son of one of the richest men of that time. But it was a big problem for Jacob. Although his father was also very rich, Jacob was many miles from home. He was also a fugitive—on the run for his life. So even though he came from a very rich home, it did him no good.

As Eliezer had looked over the girls at the well he had asked God for a specific sign to show him which one was the best. "Lord, let the young woman who is the right one for Isaac agree not only to give me a drink, but to get water for my camels as well," he had prayed.

But Jacob, who must have known this story very well, asked for no such sign. He didn't even ask the first girl he saw for a drink. Instead, when he saw a beautiful girl come along he offered to help her get the water she needed.

"May I ask your name?" Jacob asked as he pulled bucket after bucket of water from the well.

"My name is Rachel, daughter of Laban," came the answer.

Rachel must have looked closely at Jacob, for a strange little smile was playing across his face. She might not have felt attracted to him, this stranger who hadn't had a chance to bathe or trim his hair. He looked like what he was—a dusty traveler wearing worn-out sandals and even more worn-out clothes. But Jacob loved Rachel from the moment he saw her. She was beautiful, gentle, and sweet. No doubt her courteous and thoughtful ways reminded him of his mother.

"And who are you?" Rachel's gentle voice broke into his thoughts.

"I am Jacob, son of Isaac and Rebekah. My mother is your father's sister, so you are my cousin."

Her eyes must have popped open at that news. "Just a minute. I'll go tell my father," she said and hurried away to tell Laban and the rest of her family the news that a cousin had come from a far distance. Jacob was immediately invited home for supper, and what a supper that was! Most likely it was the first decent, home-cooked meal he had eaten in weeks, and possibly even months.

Unlike Eliezer, Jacob did not state his business right away. While he had come to find a wife and make his home among his mother's people, he was also running for his life. But the sad details of his story leaked out, over time.

No doubt Laban, who later turned out to be a greedy and deceptive fellow, remembered the

riches that Eliezer had brought when he came in search of Rebekah.

"Have Isaac and Rebekah fallen on hard times?" Laban must have wondered. "Why is a son of Isaac coming to me like this, with only the coat on his back?"

Laban liked Jacob though. In the few weeks that Jacob stayed as a guest in Laban's home, Jacob proved himself to be a very hard worker. So Laban offered to give Jacob a job working for him. This led them into a little discussion about what Jacob's wages would be, which finally gave Jacob the opportunity to say what he had wanted to say so badly.

"I will work seven years for you for the hand of your daughter Rachel," Jacob told Laban. By now Rachel must have guessed that Jacob thought she was very special. Perhaps he drew water for her flocks every day, or helped her gather sticks for a fire, or was quick to lift the curtain door of any tent if she even remotely considered going into it.

Laban liked Jacob, and it seems safe to say that Rachel liked him too. So the agreement was made, and Jacob started working for Laban. Today seven years seems like a long time to wait for a marriage, but the Bible has something very sweet to say about Jacob and Rachel. It says that those seven years "seemed like only a few days to him because of his love for her" (Genesis 29:20).

CHAPTER 8

The Meanest Trick in the Bible

During the seven years that Jacob worked for Rachel, you can be sure that he spent all the time he could getting to know her. Perhaps after he came in from a long day in the fields they took a walk by the river, or ate supper together, or just sat in the corner of Laban's tent and talked.

By now Rachel probably already knew about her Aunt Rebekah, and how God had chosen her to be the "mother of many nations." Now Rachel would get to be part of God's wonderful plan. Perhaps someday she would even get to meet Aunt Rebekah, since God had promised to take Jacob safely back to the land of his father. As the seven years flew by, Jacob and Rachel worked out the many ways they would make their home happy, how it would ring with the voices of their many children, and how their home would be a blessing to all the people around.

But life—and people—can be cruel sometimes. It was the custom in Laban's culture that the older daughter must be married before the younger one. When Jacob first asked to marry Rachel, this hadn't seemed like a problem. Laban had seven whole years to find Leah a husband, and that seemed like a long time.

But now the time had come for Jacob to marry Rachel, and Leah was still unmarried. The Bible says that she had weak eyes. Whatever the problem, she wasn't the girl Jacob had loved at first sight, and Laban was afraid no man would want to marry her. Leah may have been a good cook, clever with weaving, and blessed with a wonderful personality, but somehow she was not seen as being very pretty or attractive.

Then Laban came up with what seemed to him a brilliant idea. He would trick Jacob by giving him Leah to marry instead of Rachel. This would solve a couple of problems for Laban. He knew that Jacob was too honorable to divorce Leah once they were married, so she would have a husband. And who knew—maybe Laban could get another seven years of work out of Jacob for Rachel.

How Laban and his family pulled this off is not clear. Perhaps some of Rachel's brothers took her for a very long ride and kept her in a nearby village. We can be sure that Leah knew about the treacherous

trick, for she had to take part in it. A heavy veil covered her face during the marriage ceremony and it was dark when she and Jacob went off together. She probably didn't say much or Jacob would have recognized her voice. However it worked and whatever it took to fool Jacob, Leah pulled it off. We don't know if she was happy about it or if she was nervous and afraid. At any rate, she had no real choice. At that time fathers ruled their household. Even grown daughters had to do what he said.

What a surprise Jacob had the next morning when it grew light and he saw Leah next to him in his tent! We think of Jacob as a courteous, kind, and thoughtful man, but this time he lost his temper. What a dirty, low-down trick this was! Jacob stomped right over to Laban's tent to give him a piece of his mind.

He'll get over it, Leah must have thought. *He must. We are married now, and Jacob will learn to love me.* Perhaps she had been jealous all along as Jacob showered his attentions on Rachel. Or maybe Leah understood why he loved her sister, even though she loved him as well.

It surely wasn't fair to Leah to be married to a man who didn't want her, and Jacob did not get over it. He had loved Rachel from the start. He had always wanted Rachel, and that was that.

Laban was waiting for Jacob. He knew he would come. And Laban, who saw no reason to apologize, drove a hard bargain.

"You can still marry Rachel," he told his steaming son-in-law. "Just wait until after the weeklong wedding celebration. A week isn't long to wait," he may have reminded Jacob. "Not after waiting seven years."

In the end, Jacob gave in. It would disgrace Leah to divorce her, and in spite of the horrible trick that had been played on him, Jacob was too honorable to do that. But it was Rachel he wanted, and there was only one way to get her.

You see, Laban had one more trick up his sleeve. "Just one week from now and you'll have Rachel," he assured Jacob. "But, of course, you must work another seven years for me!"

What a terrible turn of events this was—all in the space of a week! Perhaps Laban felt it was OK to trick Jacob because Jacob had tricked his own father. Perhaps as the years had passed, Jacob had gotten too busy to talk to God or to listen for His voice. Maybe if God had been an important part of Jacob's life, God would have warned him about what was about to happen. Whatever the case, this trickery is just one more example of the truth of that time-tested saying "What goes around comes around."

Jacob had lied to his father, and now his uncle and substitute bride had lied to him. It was bitter medicine, this thread of dishonesty, that Jacob would face again as his life went on.

CHAPTER 9

The Great Baby Derby

After the emotional uproar that they had been through, you can be sure that Jacob and Rachel were thrilled when Leah's bridal week was up and *they* could finally get married. However, there was a taint to the wedding and the feasting. All the hopes and dreams that Jacob and Rachel had shared were now blasted to bits by having to share their home with Leah.

Jacob loved God and he meant to do right, but being tricked into having two wives instead of one—and being married to someone he really didn't love—would be a lot for any man to take. The Bible, which never minces words on such topics, puts it plainly: "Leah was despised" (Genesis 29:31, Amplified).

It was a bitter pill for the twosome-become-threesome, a problem that caused tears and regret for many more years to come. How the angels, peeking out of the portals of heaven, must have sighed at the whole situation. "If that doesn't beat all!" you can just hear them saying. "Abraham made a mess of things with Hagar, and Jacob's deception of Isaac didn't do him any good. And now there's the constant bickering between Rachel and Leah. How can we ever put up with it if they become our neighbors?"

Things got even more interesting when Leah and Rachel became involved in a little contest that grew more important every year. At that time the job of most women was to be a wife and mother. Rachel did well at the wife part. Jacob loved her best, and she loved him dearly. But it's hard to be a mother when you don't have babies, and as year after year passed it broke Rachel's heart that she couldn't have children.

Leah, on the other hand, had baby boys left and right. The Bible tells us that God saw that Leah wasn't loved, so He helped her have babies. This whole story is a gentle reminder to us that children are a gift from the Lord. God was in control, watching over the lives of both Rachel and Leah, and He helped Leah to have babies first.

In many ways Leah's life was hard. Whatever her dreams for her marriage, it was obvious that Jacob's heart belonged to Rachel. We know that Leah felt unloved, because the Bible records what she said when each of her babies was born.

"The Lord has surely looked on my affliction,"

she said when the first baby boy came along. "Now therefore, my husband will love me" (Genesis 29:32, NKJV). And she named him Reuben.

"Because the Lord has heard that I am unloved," she said when her second baby boy, Simeon, was born, "He has therefore given me this son also" (verse 33, NKJV).

Perhaps by the time the third baby boy, named Levi, came around, Leah had given up on the idea of ever being loved. All she said at his birth was "now this time my husband will become attached to me, because I have borne him three sons" (verse 34, NKJV).

When her fourth baby, Judah, was born, Leah didn't say anything about love or attachment at all. Perhaps by this time she realized that the main source of love and strength in her life would come from God alone. No doubt she turned to Him in all her trouble, and He had become quite a friend to her.

"Now I will praise the Lord," she said after Judah was born (verse 35, NKJV).

This was all pretty hard on Rachel, who also wanted to have children very badly. Here was Leah, busy with her four darling little boys. Rachel watched Reuben, Simeon, Levi and Judah learn to walk, talk, and play out in the fields—yet she had no baby. The more Rachel watched Leah and her four little boys, the more jealous she got. It wasn't enough to be the favorite wife—she wanted children! She and Jacob even had a little spat about the whole matter.

One day Rachel couldn't stand it any longer. "Give me children," she told Jacob, "or I'm going to die!"

"Who do you think I am? God?" Jacob shot back.

"He—not I—is the one who is not letting you have a baby yet."

Then Rachel, who must have known very well all the troubles Abraham and Sarah had when Abraham added Hagar as a wife, suggested that Jacob take her maid, Bilhah, as a third wife.

"I have to share him with Leah anyway," she must have reasoned. "If Bilhah has children, I can call them mine. Then at least I will have a baby to love and mother."

Jacob took Rachel up on her offer, and the Great Baby Derby, or contest, began in earnest. Soon Bilhah was pregnant and had a son, whom Rachel called Dan.

"God has judged my case; and He has also heard my voice and given me a son," Rachel said (Genesis 30:6, NKJV). But still the tension between the two sisters went on. We know that it did because every time that a baby of theirs was born, they had something to say about it.

When Bilhah had a second baby boy, Rachel said, "I have had a great struggle with my sister, and I have won" (verse 8). She named this baby Naphtali.

Well, now that Rachel's maidservant had given her two sons, Leah was not to be outdone. Soon she, too, gave her maid to Jacob as a wife. And before long that maid, whose name was Zilpah, added two more sons to Jacob's family.

Then Leah herself had two more sons and a daughter. By then poor Leah must have given up on the idea of feeling loved, because when Zebulun, her last son, was born she didn't say anything about love. She must have thought that having six boys was an accomplishment, for she said, "This time my husband will treat me with honor, because I have borne him six sons" (verse 20).

But something else was about to happen, something that would change Jacob's household again. God answered the many years of Rachel's prayers and gave her a beautiful little boy whom she named Joseph. Rachel was overjoyed with this son of her very own, and poured all the motherly love and energy she'd been saving up for so long into her one little boy.

And Jacob, too, loved Joseph very much—more than any of his other sons.

Unfortunately, this made the unhappy home situation of Jacob and his wives much worse. Children are smart, and you can be sure that Leah's sons had quickly figured out who was the best-loved wife and, then after Joseph's birth, who was the favorite son. The hurt and bitterness that Leah had felt for so long, they also felt. They may have tried to keep it hidden, but it was there, like an open sore. And it festered and grew until one day, even though they knew right and wrong, they took a terrible revenge on their brother.

CHAPTER 10

Turbulent Times

You don't have to be a mathematician to understand the Bible, but sometimes a little math doesn't hurt. Since the stories in the Bible are lined up one after the other, it's easy to think that each happened right after the other. But many years went by between many of the stories that follow one after the other.

By looking at the details the Bible gives us about the lives of Isaac and Jacob, we learn that Jacob was about 70 years old when he left his home and everyone he knew and ran for his life from Esau. By adding up the time Jacob stayed with Laban, we see it was 20 years. The first seven years he worked for the hand of Rachel (though he was given Leah). Then he worked seven more years for Rachel. That makes 14 years. The last six years there he continued to work for Laban, but this time Laban paid him in cattle.

Now remember, Jacob worked for seven years before he was married. Twenty minus 7 equals 13. Most of Jacob's children were born before he and Laban parted ways about 13 years later, and when we add up the number of children each wife had, we find it was 11.

These 13 years should have been a happy time for Jacob, with all those childish voices ringing through his tents and all those little boys running around. But in addition to all the quarreling between his wives, Jacob had plenty of other troubles as well.

Jacob's father-in-law, Laban, was a pretty slick businessman. He was always looking out for number one, which just happened to be him. The first tangle between Laban and Jacob was over the lie about Leah. Unfortunately for Jacob that was only the beginning.

During the first seven years that Jacob worked for Rachel's hand in marriage, Laban was supposed to be laying aside Jacob's wages as a wedding present to the couple. That was the custom of the day, and was a father's way of getting the newlyweds off to a good financial start. But the Bible says that Laban kept that money for himself.

Then there was the little matter of exactly what Jacob's wages were. Laban and Jacob had an agreement that Laban would pay Jacob in cattle. Jacob chose cows of a certain color, such as brown or speckled, and whatever calves of that color were born were to belong to Jacob. God, who blessed

Jacob in whatever he did, made sure that many of the new calves were the color that would go to Jacob. Laban noticed this, so he kept changing the color of cows that Jacob would get. Over a six-year period Laban changed what he was paying Jacob 10 times!

Finally Jacob, who was a very patient man, had had quite enough. He had stayed with Laban a long time because he was afraid of Esau. But 20 long years had come and gone. Surely by now Esau would have cooled off a bit. As Jacob thought about these things, God came to him in a dream.

"You can go back to the land of your father now," God told Jacob. "Do not be afraid, for I will be with you."

Before making the final decision to leave Laban, Jacob did one more thing. He asked Rachel and Leah to meet with him in the fields away from the family tents where Laban could not hear them talk. Jacob wasn't sure how Laban would feel about him leaving with all the cows, sheep, and other livestock he had gotten during his stay. In fact, he was sure that Laban would try to stop him. He thought he might have to leave quietly, and wanted to see how Rachel and Leah felt about it.

For once Rachel and Leah agreed. They had seen how Laban had treated Jacob. They probably had heard the talk from their own brothers who weren't friendly to Jacob anymore and even felt afraid. Their own lives had been made very bitter by Laban's lying ways. The Bible doesn't say much about it, but Leah probably had not had any choice when Laban had told her to trick Jacob. He may have told her at the last minute, and she may have been afraid of what he would do to her if she didn't obey. In any case, their father had caused plenty of trouble for them—right down to keeping their money.

"Our father treats even us like strangers," Rachel and Leah told Jacob. "He sold us to you and then kept the money he was supposed to give us. If it were up to him, we would not get any inheritance. The things you have gotten—they belong to us and our children. So whatever God told you to do, let's do it."

Jacob, who had had a little experience in running for his life before, waited for just the right moment to go. When Laban and his sons were away on a trip, Jacob packed up everything and left as quickly as he could. Jacob had a three-day head start before Laban even knew he was gone. It took Laban seven days to catch up with him.

Even though Jacob had earned everything he had, Laban still thought of it all as his. It's likely that Laban planned to hurt Jacob or at least force him to come back because God stepped in with a dream.

"Be careful how you treat Jacob," God warned Laban. "Do not say anything good or bad to him."

That kept Laban from hurting Jacob, but didn't keep him from showing his anger when he finally caught up with him. "What in the world do you think you are doing?" he demanded. "You sneaked away while I was gone and took my daughters like they were prisoners of war. Why did you go secretly? You didn't even give me time to throw a party, or kiss my children and grandchildren. You have been very foolish," Laban went on. "I could hurt you right now, but the God of your fathers came to me in a dream and told me that I should not."

Laban's speech was the last straw for Jacob. "What is my crime?" he demanded. "What sin have I done to you that you chased me down the way you did?"

He didn't give Laban a chance to reply before he went on. "I worked for you with all my heart for 20 years. If one of your sheep was lost or stolen, you made me pay for it. I went without sleep many times. I was thirsty and cold and tired, but I still took care of your sheep. But you were anything but fair with me. You changed my wages 10 times, and if God hadn't set you straight last night, you would be trying to take everything I have. God saw how you treated me, and gave you a scolding last night."

Laban knew it was useless to argue. He couldn't do anything to Jacob because God wouldn't let him. It was time to make peace and move on. So he said some peaceful things to Jacob, and the two of them agreed to part ways as friends. They made a promise to each other to live in peace, and even set up a pillar of rocks as a monument to the special occasion.

Then Jacob offered a sacrifice to God, and they all had a very special meal together. The next morning Laban got up and kissed Rachel, Leah, and all his grandchildren goodbye. The Bible records a number of things that Jacob and Laban said to each other before their final goodbye, and no doubt quite a few things were said that were not recorded. But one thing Laban said has echoed down through time. Thousands of years later people still use Laban's words when they say goodbye: "May the Lord watch between you and me when we are absent one from another" (Genesis 31:49, NKJV).

So Jacob and his family, through the providence of God, were able to leave in peace after all. The fussing and feuding with Laban was behind him. Jacob was headed home at last—home to the land of his father.

CHAPTER 11

In the Grip of God

At long last Jacob was free from the clutches of Laban. God had blessed him, but he had also worked hard and managed his money so carefully that he was a wealthy man. Although he had the birthright, he didn't need his father's riches. He was the first "father of many nations" to have a bundle of children. And he was headed home—home to see his father and, he hoped, his beloved mother again. But there was one nagging thought that just wouldn't stay out of his mind. When, and if, he saw Isaac and Rebekah, he would surely see Esau, too. The problem was, he still didn't want to see Esau. Fear of Esau had been what had led him to leave his homeland in the first place.

"Have I escaped Laban only to be killed by Esau?" Jacob asked himself. "What if Esau hasn't cooled off?" Even though God had promised to be with him and bring him safely back to the land of his father, Jacob still had moments when he felt nearly overcome by fear.

Even after 20 years Jacob was well aware that the horrible lie he'd told his father was the reason for his exile from home. He still felt very guilty, so guilty that thoughts of his unworthiness plagued him day and night. Jacob should have felt happy when the hills of his homeland first came into view over the horizon. Instead, fear filled his heart. He wondered if Esau would think he had come home just to get his share of all the things Isaac owned.

Then God sent Jacob a special sign to let him know, once again, that He was with him on this journey, and always. As Jacob got nearer and nearer to home he saw two armies of angels. They were God's angels, sent to protect him and his family as they traveled. One of the armies went ahead of Jacob's caravan to clear the way. The other protected the rear.

Jacob was so impressed that he gave that place a special name, Mahanaim, which means two camps. "Mahanaim" reminded Jacob of the two camps of angels surrounding him and his family as they traveled. How wonderful God had been to send two whole armies of angels to Jacob just when he needed it most! And God will do the same for each of us when we need Him, for the Bible says that "the angel of the Lord encamps around those who fear him, and he delivers them" (Psalm 34:7).

But even though God was with Jacob, guiding and protecting him every step of the way, he still felt as though he himself should do something to keep his family safe.

"Take a friendly message to my brother," Jacob told his servants. "When you give him my message, be sure to call him 'my lord' and tell him that I am 'his servant, Jacob.' Let him know that I have many sheep, cows and servants of my own, just in case he thinks that I will try to take his things."

Jacob's entire camp waited and wondered as the servants delivered the gifts. What would Esau say? Would he forgive Jacob and live peacefully with his brother?

When Jacob's servants finally returned to camp they didn't have to say a word. The fear written all over their faces told the whole story. There was no friendly message from Esau.

"Esau is on his way right now," they gasped, "with 400 armed men!"

Rachel and Leah winced at the look on Jacob's face. So did Reuben, Simeon, and the rest of Jacob's family. No doubt little Joseph clung to Rachel's skirts, wondering how he could hide. Judah and the older boys, just barely into their teens, started thinking of places to run to or ways to defend themselves. Soon the whole camp was nearing a fearful uproar.

What can I do? Jacob wondered. He could not go back, yet he was afraid to move forward. Quickly he divided out three generous gifts for his brother. Next he organized his entire camp into two bands so that if one was attacked the other might have a chance to escape.

Then Jacob did the only thing left for him to do, the thing that every one of us should do when we get ourselves into a jam. He spent time alone with God. On a lonely night in a quiet spot, Jacob finally poured out his heart to God in a way he'd never done before. Having sent his family on ahead, he was in the mountains alone by the river Jabbok. It was a dangerous area where murders and robberies often took place. But Jacob wasn't thinking of his own safety so much as that of his wives and children. The thought that his entire family might lose their lives weighed him down like a ton of bricks. Even worse than that was the awful fact that his own terrible sin had caused all of this trouble.

CHAPTER 12

The Muscle That Shrank

It was Jacob who had tricked his father and made Esau angry so many years before. He was the guilty one, yet his innocent children could very soon pay for his crime. Jacob felt so bad about it all that a torrent of salty tears washed down his cheeks as he cried and prayed out loud to God.

Suddenly, just after midnight, Jacob felt a strong hand on his shoulder. He didn't bother to ask who it was—he thought he knew who it was. He thought that someone had heard his cries to God and had come to rob or kill him. The night was pitch-black. He couldn't see, and he was too afraid to speak.

Instead he began a desperate wrestling match, pitting muscle against muscle, grip against grip, strength against strength.

Jacob was getting old in years, but he was still strong. Years of working in the fields had built a body that, though aging, was muscular and tough. But he needed every ounce of strength he could muster to fight this unknown stranger.

As Jacob battled for his physical life, he fought for his spiritual life as well. His sins rose up before him, growing into a mighty mountain in his anguished mind. But he did not give up. He did not let up, not for an instant. And so the wrestling went on. With his body he fought for his life, while in his mind he pleaded with God for mercy, forgiveness, and a fresh new start.

The wrestling match went on for hours. The sun had just begun to break between two mountains when the stranger freed one hand and touched Jacob's thigh. That one touch gave Jacob a clue as to whom he'd been wrestling all night long. A muscle in Jacob's thigh suddenly got smaller—in fact, it shrank. Instantly Jacob was in horrible pain. He would limp on that leg for the rest of his earthly life.

When Jacob realized that he had been wrestling with Jesus Himself, he held on all the more tightly. What had gone on for hours as a wrestling match now became a clinging contest. Jacob refused to let go without a blessing. So, though exhausted and in terrible pain, he hung on for dear life.

Jesus tried to wrench Himself free. "Let Me go, for it's just about sunrise," He said.

"I will not let You go unless You bless me" came

back the anguished reply. Jacob was not being proud or sassy by refusing to let go of Jesus. God knew his heart. If he had been, he would have been instantly punished. No, Jacob was simply claiming the promises of God. He was truly humble, he was sorry for his sin, and most of all, he had surrendered his heart fully to God. Though his hands trembled, he had the promises of God firmly in his grip. And God (who loves every one of us as much as He loved Jacob) could not turn away the sinner's plea. This is why the Bible tells us that Jacob "had power over the angel, and prevailed" (Hosea 12:4, KJV).

All his life Jacob had run ahead of God, taking things into his own hands. Now he realized just how bad that was. As never before, he saw that he needed to trust God fully and that God would take care of things—in His time. He asked God for forgiveness, and God forgave Jacob.

"Your name will be changed," Jesus told Jacob. "Your new name will be Israel, because you are a prince who has power with God and with man, and have prevailed."

The name Jacob means someone who pushes others out of the way and takes their place. But the name Israel means prince. From a "supplanter" to a "prince"—what a change, what a transformation! In that awful night of wrestling Jacob learned to trust God in a way he had never trusted before, and he was blessed for it.

The story of Jacob wrestling by the river is especially important for those of us living in the last days of earth when the clock is ticking down. Through the prophet Jeremiah, God says that people living just before Jesus comes will go through a hard time, just as Jacob did. But He also says that we, like Jacob, will be saved out of it.

"Cries of fear are heard—terror, not peace. . . .

"How awful that day will be! None will be like it.

"It will be a time of trouble . . . , but he will be saved out of it" (Jeremiah 30:5-7).

Satan had tried to discourage Jacob. He was happy to point out Jacob's sins and try to tear Jacob away from God. He had inspired Esau to bring 400 men and march toward Jacob's family with intentions of killing every one of them.

When Jesus wrestled with Jacob, God didn't really want Jesus to get away. When He tried to escape, He was just testing Jacob's faith. God wanted to know just how strong that faith really was, for faith is like a muscle. When it gets a lot of exercise, it gets stronger. And that's what God wanted for Jacob.

At the end of time, enemies of God's people will want to kill them. Satan will try to discourage them by pointing out their sins. God Himself may test their faith from time to time, to help make it stronger. But all who hold on to God like Jacob did, who claim the promises, trust God, and never give up, can have the victory.

Those who are not willing to give up every sin, or who will not spend the time to get hold of God's blessing, will lose the war. But if we get a grip on God's promises the way Jacob did, we can be sure that success will be ours. God loves to give good things to His children, but He is waiting for us to ask. When we ask God for something that we know is His will, He wants us to be persistent—not because He needs us to bug Him continually before He will give us anything, but because our persistence shows how badly we really want it.

Sometimes, when children ask for something good, they think their parents don't hear them. But the parents may be waiting to make sure that what their children asked for is something they truly want. We appreciate things so much more when we really do want them. That's the way it is with God's promises. You must truly want them, then claim them for yourself. Get God's promises in your grip and never let go.

Reach out and grab one today.

CHAPTER 13

Esau Gets the Message

It's amazing how God works for a praying Christian, even before they are aware that God is answering their prayer. That's what happened with Jacob. Even as he was wrestling with Jesus, God was busy sending Esau a dream.

As it turned out, Jacob and his family had every reason to be worried. Esau was on his way to meet Jacob with 400 armed men, and they weren't a welcome committee. Esau had no intention of forgiving his brother. Rather, he planned to settle the score.

That's when God took over in a way that only He can. If we want to get a message to someone, we might call, e-mail or even text-message them the words we want them to hear. But God has so many other ways to get our attention and He uses them all. In Bible times He made a donkey talk, He made fire fall out of heaven, and His voice thundered off a mountaintop. Sometimes He sent angels to carry His messages, but He was also known to use an army of frogs, a million hornets, and oh, yes, He often used dreams.

Esau wasn't a praying man so he wasn't exactly asking for God's advice. But God had some advice for him anyway. In his dream, Esau saw how hard it had been on Jacob to be away from home for 20 long years. He saw Jacob's heartbreak when he learned that his mother was dead. He also saw the armies of God surrounding Jacob's camp.

Esau may have been a hardened soul, but God spoke, and he got the message. The next morning he gave his soldiers a good talking-to. "I know this might seem strange to you," he told them, "because I planned to kill my brother, Jacob, and all of his family. But last night the God of my father came to me in a dream."

"You are not to hurt Jacob," Esau went on. "And neither will I. Do not harm him or his family, or his servants in any way."

At last the long-awaited moment came, when the two groups came in sight of each other. On the one hand was Esau the desert chieftain, armed to the teeth with all of his soldiers. On the other side stood Jacob, the prince of God, who would be called Israel from this moment on. Though pale and exhausted from the struggle the night before, though limping and in pain from the injury he had received, joy and peace filled his face.

Esau ran to meet his brother and what a reunion

they had! The twins, who had tussled even before they were born, were at peace with each other at last. The Bible tells us that "Esau ran to meet Jacob . . . ; he threw his arms around his neck and kissed him. And they wept" (Genesis 33:4).

What a tender picture of brotherly love! What a change for them both! This was especially true for Esau, who less than a day before had meant to kill Jacob. Even Esau's soldiers, rude and rough as they were, were touched by the emotion of it all. Though they knew about Esau's dream, the change in their leader was nothing short of amazing. Esau had gone from being a man who was bitter and vengeful to someone who was genuinely happy to see his brother. God really does change hearts!

At some point Esau must have broken it to Jacob that their mother was dead, and they cried once again together. After catching up on all the family news and having a good visit, Jacob and Esau knew it was time to part. They could visit each other from time to time, but their lives were too different and their families too big, for them to live together.

"I'll travel with you on the way back home," Esau told him. "We will protect you, and get you to Father's house."

"That's OK." Jacob wasn't worried. He remembered the armies of angels who had surrounded his family before. "Your army will go too fast for my sheep, lambs, and the little children. Thanks for the offer, but you can go on ahead. We will follow as fast as we can."

So once again the twin brothers said goodbye. It was so much different from their parting 20 years before. After nearly a hundred years of fussing and feuding, the tussle of the twins was finally over.

CHAPTER 14

The Sad, Bad Story of Shechem

In addition to his 12 sons, Jacob had a daughter named Dinah. The Bible doesn't say much about her, though it does tell one very sad story that happened when she was a teenager.

The Bible says that Dinah went out to "see the daughters of the land" (Genesis 34:1, KJV). This turned out not to be a wise decision. While Christians should always try to be a witness to those who don't love God, there is danger in going to the parties of those who are far from Him. There may be wine served, or there may be other things that could influence a Christian away from God. It pays to be careful, as Dinah found out the hard way.

Evidently when Dinah went out to see the daughters of the land, she met up with at least one of the sons of the land as well. His name and the name of the town where he lived were both Shechem. In many ways, Shechem was an honorable young man. But despite whatever good points he had, he was also used to the heathen customs of his town. When he took a liking to Dinah, he didn't think twice about taking her home and acting as if she were his wife. If they had been married this would have been fine, but the problem was, they weren't.

When Dinah's brothers found out about this they were extremely angry. More than that, they wanted to get revenge on the young man who'd taken advantage of their sister.

Shechem didn't have a clue about that, however. He had fallen in love with Dinah and wanted very badly to marry her.

"See if you can arrange a wedding," Shechem said to his father.

This was exactly the opening that Simeon and Levi, two of Jacob's oldest—and cruelest—sons, were hoping for. They agreed that Shechem could marry Dinah, but they were using the marriage agreement to get revenge. And they made sure that their father didn't know what they were up to. They felt certain he would spoil their plans.

So Simeon and Levi made a deal with Shechem and his father. If all the men in the town of Shechem would agree to give a sign of their approval of the marriage, then the wedding would take place. There was a serious catch, however. What they asked the men of Shechem to do was painful. But when the men all talked it over, they agreed because it meant that they, too, might find wives among the camp of Jacob.

"When they're very sore and don't feel like fighting we'll go in and kill them," Levi and Simeon promised each other. And that's exactly what they did. They killed all the men, and cruel as they were, they took all the weeping wives and children as captives.

Jacob was filled with horror when he learned what his own sons had done.

"You have made me and our whole camp stink in the land," he shouted. "Before you know it, they will band together to take revenge. Then our whole family—and the whole camp—will be completely wiped out."

Simeon and Levi didn't care. "There is no way that guy was going to get away with what he did" was all they said.

It hurt Jacob to see the cruelty and dishonesty of his own sons. It was time for a real revival in the camp. Through his experiences, Jacob himself had finally come to know God truly, but somehow his sons did not know Him at all. They were even bringing idols into the camp. Just when Jacob was feeling really bad about all this, he got a message from God.

"Go down to Bethel and offer a sacrifice there."

A warm glow came over Jacob when he thought of Bethel. Bethel was where God had visited him in a dream when he was a much younger man, running away from Esau. Bethel was where he had seen the angels going up and down the steps to heaven. Yes, Bethel was just what his family needed right now.

"We need to get back to God," Jacob told his family. Then, with heartfelt emotion, he told the story of how God had led in his life. He told how he had left his father's tent as a lonely wanderer, running for his life. He told how God had sent him the dream at Bethel. And he told how God had watched over and cared for him every day of his life.

As Jacob told his story, or testimony, to his family, his own heart was touched and softened by the wonderful love of God. His sons, bitter and hardened as some of them were, were also deeply moved by the wonderful story.

"Put away your false gods," Jacob told them. And they did. More than that, they all joined Jacob at the family altar in Bethel, as they asked God to forgive them and help them start over again. God answered their prayer, and He also made the people of Canaan afraid of the sons of Jacob, so that no one tried to take revenge for their bloody deed.

But in spite of his joy at the spiritual revival of his family, the next few days were sad for Jacob and his family. Deborah, who had been Rebekah's nurse when she was a child, was laid to rest at Bethel. This faithful servant, who had first traveled with Rebekah when she went to marry Isaac, and later found a home with Jacob after he came back to Canaan, had been a special reminder to Jacob of the happy times with his mother.

Just a few days after Jacob buried Deborah, his beloved Rachel died while giving birth to her second child. In truth, Jacob had worked 14 years for the hand of Rachel. She was the one he loved, and now she was gone.

After all of this trouble, Jacob was glad when, at last, he reached the home of his father, Isaac. And

Isaac, who was old, blind, and lonely, was glad to see Jacob too. Esau was around, but it was Jacob who spent time with and comforted his elderly father during the last years of Isaac's life. When Isaac did die, Jacob generously gave Esau all of his father's wealth. Jacob was happy to have the spiritual birthright—it was what he had really wanted all along. This was fine with Esau, because the money was all that mattered to him.

CHAPTER 15

Hope in the Middle of the Muddle

As we read about Jacob we see that he had a lot of trouble in his life. First there was the lie he told his father, and the terrible price he paid in having to run for his life. Then there was the trick played on him by Laban and Leah. That lying trick led to Jacob having two wives and continual quarreling in his home. There was the frightening time Esau and his army marched toward Jacob and he feared for his life. Then the night Jacob spent wrestling with Jesus, and the lifelong limp he received during that wrestling match.

But worst of all, in his old age Jacob was shamed and grieved by the evil done by his very own sons. As if that weren't enough, he was heartbroken when he learned that his mother was dead. He felt crushed at the death of his beloved Rachel, and devastated by the deaths of Deborah and Isaac. Jacob lived a long life, and if you put all his troubles close together they would be enough to overwhelm just about anybody.

Of course, there were many happy times in Jacob's life too. He had been blessed with a good father and a godly mother. He felt blessed to be married to Rachel whom he loved more than anything, and Leah did what she could to be a good wife too.

And one of the brightest times in Jacob's life was the birth of Joseph, his eleventh son and Rachel's firstborn. Those were wonderful years, when little Joseph was a child learning to walk and talk. He loved his father and was the light of Jacob's life.

Joseph was a handsome boy, but that's not the reason Jacob loved Joseph best. There was something different about Joseph. From the time he was small he listened to his father's instruction and wanted to do what was right. Compared to the way Jacob's other sons acted, he found that being with Joseph made his heart glad.

Even as a young boy, Joseph loved God very much. No doubt his mother, Rachel, told him how his great-grandfather Abraham and his grandfather Isaac had been called by God to father a great nation. Even though Joseph was only 4 years old when Rachel died, those four years were very important. You can be sure that she did everything she could to get Joseph's character off to a good start, and she did a very good job.

After his mother died, Joseph clung even more

closely to his father. The beautiful traits of character that would someday make Joseph a strong leader were already starting to blossom. Jacob noticed them right away. Joseph was respectful to his father and obeyed what he said. He loved God and loved to obey Him. He was honest, gentle, and faithful. No wonder Jacob "loved Joseph more than any of his other sons" (Genesis 37:3).

Of course, it is one thing for a parent to feel that extra bit of love for one child; it is another to show it. From his own bitter experience with Esau, Jacob should have known better. It's bad for a parent to plainly favor one child above the other. Then too, Jacob's home and the lives of his older sons had been badly hurt by the jealousy between Leah and Rachel. Unfortunately, that jealousy carried down to their children. But Jacob wasn't thinking of that.

While Jacob's other sons gave him trouble, Joseph obeyed. While his other sons had a mean streak, Joseph was thoughtful and kind. It was easy to be with Joseph, easy to care for Joseph, easy for Jacob to love him more than the rest. *Besides,* he reasoned, *Joseph's mother is dead. He needs me.*

"I'm going to make you a very special coat," Jacob told Joseph. It was the kind of coat that only princes wore in those days. Joseph was a good-looking young man in regular clothes so you can be sure that he really turned heads when he put on that expensive, finely-made coat. Unfortunately, some of the heads he turned were those of his brothers. Soon the evil monster of jealousy, which had lived in Jacob's camp for so long, reared its ugly head once again.

"Just look at that coat!" Joseph's brothers whispered between clenched teeth. "Father never made one of us a coat like that."

"Do you think that means he wants to give Joseph the birthright?" another asked.

Reuben, son of Leah, was Jacob's oldest boy. But Reuben had already been involved in some very evil living, and Jacob was deeply disappointed in him. Of course, because Jacob had been tricked into marrying Leah, he probably thought of Rachel as his real wife. And he'd think of Joseph as the firstborn son, the one in line for the birthright that, as a young man, Jacob himself had wanted so badly.

To make matters worse, Joseph had two dreams that seemed to say that his father, mother, and 11 brothers would someday bow down to him. In his innocence Joseph told them all about the dream. He never considered that his brothers already hated him and would be furious at the idea that they'd bow down to him. But even Jacob, who loved Joseph with all his heart, asked, "What is this dream you had? Will your mother and I and your brothers actually come and bow down to the ground before you?" (Genesis 37:10).

As Joseph grew into his midteens Jacob sent him to help his brothers who tended the flocks of sheep and goats in pastures a long way from home. It was there that Joseph got a glimpse of what his brothers were actually like. While they were around their father, the wayward young men put on an act of being the kind of sons their dad wanted them to be. But out of his sight they could be themselves—crude, dishonest, with little respect for their father or for God.

Joseph saw all this, and it really tore at his heart. He loved God, and wanted his brothers to love and serve God too. So he reported the bad things they were doing to Jacob. You can imagine how mad that made them! Now as well as being a show-off, they told each other, Joseph was a tattletale. They didn't want him around at all.

Joseph was probably better looking than his brothers, which made them jealous. He was the favorite son of the favorite wife—and they weren't. He had these annoying dreams, not to mention an irritating fashion statement of a coat. The very fact that he did what was right while they did what they knew was wrong was a constant thorn in their side.

When Joseph had eagerly told them his dreams, his face had shone with the light of God, but that made them all the madder. Instead of stopping to think that they should turn their lives around, they hated their brother all the more. Then there was this little matter of him telling on them to their father. They were embarrassed and ashamed that their sins had been found out, but they still had no intention to change.

So it was that while Joseph was growing up, innocently doing what he knew to be right, his brothers grew to dislike him more and more. What started as just a little "pimple" of dislike grew and festered until it was an open sore—a sore spot of jealousy, hate, and rage that would soon be shown in a shocking and terribly vengeful way.

CHAPTER 16

Down but Not Out

By this time Jacob was quite a rich man. He had so many sheep that it was hard to find enough good pasture to graze them all. When the flocks had eaten all the grass in one area they had to be moved to another grassy place where there was plenty for them to eat. As you know, Jacob and his big family and all their servants and helpers lived in tents. They were much bigger than today's camping tents and were furnished with carpets, pillows, and a few other things. It was a lot of work to take down, roll up, and move the tents for all those people. So while the sheep were moved here and there to find good grass, Jacob's family stayed where they were.

When this story begins, Jacob's 10 oldest sons had taken the flock to Shechem. They'd been gone for several months and Jacob was worried. You'll remember that not many years before Simeon and Levi had murdered all the men in the town of Shechem. Jacob was afraid that other tribes had taken revenge so he sent Joseph to find them and make sure they were OK.

Seventeen-year-old Joseph was old enough to make the trip on his own, and he must have been excited to be given such responsibility. If Jacob had had any idea how much his sons hated Joseph he would never have trusted Joseph alone with them. But by now they were experts at fooling their father. They'd led Jacob to believe that everything was fine between them and Joseph, when really they hated their brother.

It was a long 50 miles to Shechem, but Joseph probably enjoyed the trip. When he arrived, he learned that the flocks had been moved to Dothan, another 15 miles away. Now, Joseph loved his brothers even though they were unkind to him, and he was eager to see them. If he'd only known what was waiting for him he would not have hurried so quickly. But Joseph had no idea.

"Hello down there!" he called as he came over the top of a hill. As tired as he was, he broke into a run when he finally saw his brothers' camp. No doubt he expected to be warmly hugged and greeted when he finally reached their camp.

They'd seen him coming, however, and they were not happy. "Here comes that dreamer!" one said to the other. "Come on. Let's kill him and throw him into one of these pits." (These pits, called cisterns, had been dug to collect water.)

"Yeah, we can say a ferocious animal got to him before he ever found us," another said.

"Then," another said angrily, "we'll see what becomes of his dreams."

Then Reuben objected. "'Let's not take his life,' he said. 'Don't shed any blood. Throw him into this cistern here in the desert, but don't lay a hand on him'" (Genesis 37:21, 22). The others shrugged. Whatever. Just so they rid themselves of the little brat for good.

Over time the little plant of dislike they had for their brother had grown into a massive tree of hatred. The roots of that tree were solid and deep, the branches wicked and cruel, and the trunk was so massive that it could hardly be moved.

Joseph never saw it coming. Tired, sweaty, hungry, and glad to find them at last, he was shocked when rough hands grabbed and held him while others ripped off his beautiful coat.

"Take that, you dreamer!" his brothers shouted.

"What's going on? What's the matter?" Joseph tried to protest. "Father sent me to—" but a slap across his face stopped his words. He felt himself dragged across the ground, then lifted and shoved. Down he went, down to the bottom of a deep, damp pit.

Joseph couldn't believe what had just happened. "Hey, let me out of here!" he called. "This isn't funny." He'd just walked 65 miles to find his brothers. He was happy to see them. What was the matter with them? Was this a bad joke?

Perhaps he let himself sink down to the muddy

floor of the pit, glad, at last, to rest his legs. He could have cried—if he hadn't been 17, and much too old for that. He was confused and scared. When would his brothers get over their anger and let him out? "Please, God . . ." he prayed. "Please."

But Joseph's brothers were not "getting over" it. Instead they had a loud discussion about whether or not to kill him. They were close enough that he heard every word, and before long he knew one thing for sure. Whether they killed him or left him there to starve to death, they would never let him go back to his father.

"The little snitch told on us before," they sneered. "You can be sure he'd tell Father about this—and that's the last thing we need."

At last their voices dropped to normal, and Joseph heard sounds that told him they were sitting down to eat. Minutes passed; then Joseph's brothers saw a caravan of Ishmaelites coming over the horizon and got a wicked idea. "Let's sell him to these traders," Judah suggested. "Then his blood won't be on our hands."

And the others agreed. "We really are nice guys after all," they laughed. "We don't really want to kill our little brother. We'll flag down the Ishmaelites and sell him to them instead."

Almost before Joseph knew what was happening, he'd been hauled up from the pit and roughly stood on his feet. A caravan of men, camels, and slaves stood nearby and stretched into the distance. In a heartbeat Joseph understood. He struggled to get away, crying and praying all at the same time, but nothing touched his brothers' hearts. They were de-

termined to get rid of him once and for all, and get a little money out of the deal as well.

Strong hands held him fast while his older brothers bargained with the caravan leader. At last money was exchanged, and Joseph was handed over to the Ishmaelites.

"How can you do this to me?" he wailed as chains were clamped around his wrists and neck to lead him away.

"Have a nice life, little brother!" Jacob's sons were laughing now, laughing at Joseph's tears. "See what all your do-gooding got you! You'll never see your beloved father—or your ridiculous coat—again."

"Oh, yeah," another shouted. "And we'll never bow down to you, either."

"You'll be the one bowing down—to your new master," hooted another, and they laughed all the harder. It was a cruel, satanic laughter, the kind of sound that people can make only when they have shut Jesus out of their heart.

Joseph sobbed and took one last look over his shoulder, hoping against hope that one of his brothers—the brothers he had loved so dearly—would show even a speck of mercy and buy him back. Then a strong Ishmaelite hand slapped his face toward the distant hills, and the awful truth began to sink in. He, who had once been an honored son, was now a slave. He could not even say goodbye to his father. And not one of his brothers would help him.

CHAPTER 17

Another Mean Lie

Reuben, Jacob's oldest son, had been away when the Ishmaelite caravan had come and bought Joseph. When he returned to camp, he didn't know Joseph was gone. In spite of his evil ways, Reuben had a sense of responsibility toward Joseph.

When my brothers aren't looking, I'll take Joseph out of the pit and send him back to our father, Reuben had thought to himself. Some of Joseph's other brothers had also felt sorry for him. But none had felt sorry enough to do anything about it. They were tough guys. They had spent many hours talking about how much they hated Joseph. They didn't want anyone to think they were sissies for not sticking with the rest. The nine brothers who had sold Joseph all felt they had gone too far to undo what they'd done. They were determined to keep with their plan, no matter what.

"Where is Joseph?" Reuben asked. "Did you send him home?"

Reuben was not only shocked, but mad at himself when he realized that Joseph was gone. "The boy isn't there! Where can I turn now?" he asked (Genesis 37:30).

As the oldest son, Reuben was expected to be the leader. He was to be the responsible one. But it seems that one wrong deed always leads to another. That is certainly the case in this story. Jacob's brothers had committed a terrible sin, and now to cover it up they had to commit another.

"If we tell Father that Joseph is lost, we'll have to spend the rest of our lives looking for him," the brothers reasoned. "Father might even trace him to wherever that caravan is going; then the whole story will come out. Father will try to buy Joseph back, and we will be cursed instead of blessed."

"As far as Father is concerned, Joseph has got to be dead," said another. "This will be very sad for him, of course. But he will get over the grief, and we can get on with our lives."

This idea made sense to them all. Even Reuben agreed. While they didn't want to hurt their father, things had gone too far not to hurt him. If they told him the truth—well, there was no telling what he would do—to them, or to himself. Besides, they'd already made up their minds. So they told him a lie, and a horrible lie at that. They told Jacob that his son was dead.

They even did something to convince him they were telling the truth. They ripped Joseph's beautiful coat, the coat decorated like that of a prince, to make it look as though there had been a struggle. Then they killed a goat from their father's flock and dipped the coat in its blood. Maybe they even rolled it in dirt to make things look more real. Then they carried the coat to their father and told him their awful lie.

Jacob had been waiting for Joseph's return and must have been glad to see his sons coming. We can know that he looked for Joseph. Maybe he asked where he was.

His sons had had several days to plan their story. "We're afraid something has happened to Joseph," one of them said as all of them tried to look concerned. "We found this coat lying by itself in a field, but we never did see the boy."

Jacob slowly took the coat they held out to him. He opened it up. The fabric was torn and covered with dried blood.

"Do you know if this is Joseph's coat, or not?" one of the sons asked.

Jacob fingered the blood-soaked stitching around the torn sleeves. His sons waited, holding their breath, to see if they'd get away with their crime. Then suddenly Jacob lifted the robe to his face and an ear-splitting howl came from his throat.

The brothers had dreaded the moment when the awful idea that Joseph was dead would dawn on their father. They had known it would be bad, but they had no idea it would be as bad as it was. The anguish, the

total grief, and the pain in their father's heartbroken face was almost more than even those hardened brothers could bear.

"It's my son's coat," Jacob sobbed. "An evil beast must have eaten him. Joseph, my son, must be ripped into pieces by now." Jacob's entire family rose up to comfort him, but he would not be comforted. He ripped his clothes and sat in rough sackcloth and ashes—the custom in those days when mourning the dead. And nothing would comfort him.

Days passed. Then weeks. Jacob wasn't hungry. He hardly ate. He withdrew into himself and didn't talk. He rocked back and forth holding Joseph's blood-soaked robe. Time is usually a healer, but it seemed to do nothing for Jacob.

"I will go down to the grave mourning for my son," he cried over and over. Rachel was gone, and now Joseph, the light of his life, was gone. Not even young Benjamin could comfort him. Joseph's death was more than Jacob could bear.

"What have we done?" the brothers asked each other when again they were out in the fields with the flocks. They were plagued by guilt and terrified by the unending grief of their father. Yet they were afraid to tell him the truth. They had thought getting rid of Joseph would solve their problems, but what had seemed so sweet in the beginning had now become very bitter.

It was bitter for Jacob, bitter for the 10 brothers, and very bitter for Joseph, who was even then on his way to Egypt to be sold as a lowly slave.

CHAPTER 18

On the Road to Egypt

Whether Joseph rode on a camel or walked to Egypt, we don't know for certain. He probably walked, for he was a slave. But however he traveled, we can be sure he had plenty of time to think. We can also be sure he went through a whole range of emotions, for his entire world had been turned upside down.

As the caravan plodded toward Egypt, it came very close to the hills of home—the hills where Joseph's father still lived and where he had spent many happy years. It was all very bitter to Joseph— to be so near, yet so far, from the home he loved and the father who had been so good to him. Joseph knew that Jacob was looking for him—waiting for him to come home. But there was no way to tell him where he was. There was no way to say what had happened.

The shock wore off, leaving Joseph terrified and overwhelmed with grief. He cried and sobbed until he thought he could cry no more, but somehow there was always one more bucket of tears waiting to pour from his bloodshot eyes.

Over and over he relived the horrible scene with his brothers. The angry faces, the cruel glares, the insults they had poured on him—it was almost more than his young heart could bear. He had begged them to change their minds, but his cries for help had met nothing but sneers. And here he was now, alone and friendless, on his way to a foreign, pagan land.

It's hard to imagine how anything good could have come out of this experience for Joseph, yet somehow it did. God has a way of turning even the very worst experiences of life into some sort of a blessing.

Although he loved his son very much, Jacob had done Joseph wrong by treating him as a favorite. The fancy, decorated coat and the many other ways Jacob showed that he favored Joseph made the other brothers angrier than they ever would have been. Though what they did was wrong—terribly cruel and wrong—Jacob had not done right either.

As a tenderly cared-for son, Joseph was not prepared for the tough times that now lay ahead. Then, too, he had a few character faults that needed to be corrected. A few days before, he had felt quite sure of himself. He didn't need anyone or anybody. He'd also gotten pretty picky when it came to dealing with other people. But in the past few hours Joseph had learned some hard lessons that could have taken him years to learn—if he would have ever learned them at all. Like it or not, he was now a slave. His freedom was gone forever. He was the lowest of the low. He would have to jump when his master said jump, or face the pain of a beating or worse.

At some point on the trip Joseph stopped crying long enough to think of his father's God, the God he had been taught to love and respect as a child. How often he had listened in his father's tent as over and over Jacob told the story of the angel-filled stairway that reached right up to the gates of heaven. How often he had heard of God's promises to Jacob, how God had always been there for his father, and how God had never let Jacob down. In his heart, Joseph believed that Jacob's God would also be his God.

Then a strange thing happened. At least it must have seemed strange to Joseph's Ishmaelite captors. The teen who had done nothing but cry, dried his tears. The look of terror left his face. His empty stare was replaced by a look of resolve, peace, and hope.

Deep in his heart Joseph had decided that the God of his father would be his God, too. He would give God 100 percent. He would be true to his faith in a heathen land, no matter the cost.

Joseph had decided also to take on a new attitude. Whatever he was asked to do, he would do it thoroughly, promptly, and as well as he could. He would be kind, courteous, and polite. He would not let himself be eaten up with bitterness.

The Ishmaelites saw only what happened on the outside. They didn't know what had gone on in Joseph's heart. But Joseph did. More fully than ever before, he had given his life to God. He was going through a very bitter experience, but instead of breaking him it had transformed him. In a few short days he had grown up. The boy had become a man.

CHAPTER 19

In Potiphar's House

H'mmm . . ." A short, chubby Egyptian squeezed Joseph's arm, then gave him a poke in the ribs. "This bloke looks like he could haul a few bricks."

An important-looking military man stepped next to the short one, taking a closer look. Joseph felt like a slab of meat being poked and prodded. But he was ready for this moment. He didn't show how he felt.

Without warning Joseph found himself sprawled on the ground. "Take that!" the military man who was Potiphar, captain of the king's guard, said with a laugh.

"Get up!" The man with rolls of fat around his naked middle kicked Joseph

in the ribs. Joseph didn't make a sound but just scrambled to his feet.

"How much do you want for that young fellow?" Potiphar asked. He casually held a small bag in his hand.

"A hundred shekels of silver," the ill-tempered Ishmaelite trader spat back.

"Ha!" Potiphar laughed out loud. "Twenty."

"That's what I paid for him, so forget it! I had to feed him all the way from Canaan—not to mention listening to him cry for three days straight."

"I don't want any crybaby."

The Ishmaelite raised an eyebrow. "Look at him now. He's a man."

"OK. Thirty-five shekels of silver."

"Seventy-five!"

"No, 40." Joseph stood quietly, eyes on the dusty ground. The haggling went on until, at last, both parties agreed on a price. Potiphar opened the small bag and counted out the pieces of silver into the merchant's hand.

"Get moving, slave." The short Egyptian, who'd stood to one side while Potiphar bargained, flicked his whip on Joseph's bare back. "We have a little job for you back at the palace." His loud, mean laugh reminded Joseph of his older brothers. But he didn't reply.

The head of Potiphar's house put the newest slave under the care of his lowest servant, who happily gave him the worst job in the palace. But Joseph did not complain or whine. He had made up his mind how to act, and with God's help, he carried through with his plan.

And as the months passed, Potiphar's servants

took note of Joseph. They learned that they didn't need to check on the rooms he swept and cleaned. They were always done well. In fact, whatever the young slave did turned out well. If he planted flowers, they grew beautifully. Given the big garden to tend, the cucumbers were bigger and sweeter, and even the onions and garlic tasted better. If he built a wall, it was straight and strong. The Egyptians didn't know what was going on. They knew there was something special about Joseph, but they didn't know why.

But Joseph knew why. Though outwardly he said little, in his heart he was serving the God of his father, and God was blessing him for it. Soon Potiphar's servants gave Joseph more and more responsibility. And whatever he did, he did well. So well, in fact, that in time Potiphar noticed Joseph himself.

"Make that young fellow my personal assistant," he said one day.

"Make that young fellow the assistant head servant," Potiphar said later. Then the time came when Potiphar made Joseph head over his entire house. Now Joseph was the boss of the obnoxious servant who'd kicked him in the ribs that first day when he stood in the market not knowing who would buy him or what would be his fate. But Joseph did not take revenge. Once again he had made up his mind how to act, and he stuck to his plan.

The Bible doesn't say how long it took for Joseph to rise through the ranks of Potiphar's slaves. Some years must have passed, for Joseph would have had to learn the language, the politics, and many other things about life in Egypt. And the Bible doesn't say how long Joseph was head over Potiphar's house.

But one terrible day Joseph's world came crashing down again.

Potiphar's wife had noticed Joseph too. It was easy to see that he was handsome and polite. She noticed that people respected him and that he had a lot of power. And so Potiphar's wife decided she wanted him for herself. Whatever the reason, the Bible says that she "cast her eyes on Joseph" (Genesis 39:7, KJV) and asked him to come be with her. She wanted him to sleep with her as if they were husband and wife. But there was a big problem. She was married to Potiphar, and Joseph knew that what she wanted was wrong.

He refused. "How then could I do such a wicked thing and sin against God?" he asked her. Joseph knew that even though we sneak around and hide things from other people, God sees everything, and He knows what we do. Joseph lived every day as though he were in the very presence of God. He didn't want to dishonor God in any way.

But day after day Potiphar's wife kept after him. As the wife of the captain of the king's guard, she was an Egyptian beauty. She may even have been tempting to Joseph. But Joseph would have nothing of it. He would not hurt Potiphar, who had been so good to him, and he would not dishonor God. Years before, Joseph had made up his mind how he would act. Nothing would change it now. He refused to be alone with this woman or to give in to her constant pleadings.

Then the fateful day came. Joseph slipped into Potiphar's house to do a chore for his master. He didn't know it, but none of the household servants were inside. Perhaps he thought Potiphar's wife was somewhere else, too, but she was there, waiting for him and more persistent than ever. Worse yet, she was angry that he wouldn't give in to her.

"Come be with me," she whispered, sneaking up behind Joseph and grabbing hold of his loose-fitting robe. Joseph whirled to get away, but she had a tight grip. She pulled the robe toward herself; he pulled the other way. Suddenly he slipped free of his cloak and ran as fast as he could from the house.

This was the last straw. She knew she would never get Joseph. Her pride was hurt. *How can he refuse me?* She was angry. *He's just a slave. He's nothing!* So she decided to hurt him back.

"Eeekkk! Help!" Her loud, shrill screams echoed through the house as she ran through the hallways, calling for her servants. They came running too. Maybe they thought that she was having a heart attack or that a robber had broken into the mansion. But to their shock she was clutching Joseph's robe in her hands and screaming that he had tried to hurt her.

It didn't take long for the servants to find him. Strong hands grabbed him and brought him back inside. It wasn't long before Potiphar was there. "How could you do this to me?" he demanded, storming into the room where his servants guarded Joseph.

"I didn't" was all Joseph said.

Potiphar shoved Joseph's cloak into his face. "Then what is the meaning of this?"

"She wouldn't let go, so I left it and ran away. I fear God, Master. I would never touch your wife."

Potiphar knew the truth. He saw it in Joseph's face and saw character. Joseph had become like a son to him. He was much more a friend than a slave. But Potiphar had his pride to deal with. He didn't want to admit that his wife was a liar. It hurt him to think she was chasing another man, and a slave at that. And so, to preserve his pride and that of his family, he gave up the best servant he ever had.

If Potiphar had really believed his wife, he would have had Joseph executed. He had the power to do it. The fact that he threw Joseph into prison showed whom Potiphar actually believed.

It was another bitter pill for Joseph to take—the third such pill in his life. The first came when he was only 4 years old, when his loving mother had died. He became a motherless child that day. The second came when he was 17, when his brothers sold him as a slave. In one moment he went from a favorite son to the lowest of the low—a slave in chains. The third came when Potiphar threw him into prison. Joseph had given his all for Potiphar. While God had blessed, Joseph had worked very hard at every task he was given.

"See where being good has gotten you," Satan whispered as Joseph was marched to the dingy prison that would now be his home. But he wasn't listening. Though discouraged and frightened, years ago Joseph had made up his mind how he would act, and he still stuck to his plan.

There may have been tears this time in the quietness of his cell. But there was also a strength that comes only from a strong trust in God. Joseph knew that God was in charge of his life. He knew that nothing could happen to him that God didn't allow to happen. And so Joseph determined to be the best, most faithful prisoner ever seen in the land of Egypt. And while he was doing that, he would wait and watch to see what God would do next.

CHAPTER 20

Joseph in Jail

Joseph paid a steep price for the lies of Potiphar's wife "They bruised his feet with shackles, his neck was put in irons, till what he foretold came to pass, till the word of the Lord proved him true" (Psalm 105:18, 19).

Being a slave had been very bad news, but rotting in an Egyptian jail was worse—much worse. Usually, prisoners were kept for only a brief time. Then they were either freed or punished. But not Joseph. As the months turned into years, somehow Joseph kept his courage and faith in God. Far from his father and younger brother, forsaken and apparently forgotten by those who ruled Egypt, Joseph knew that the God of heaven was still on His throne. He knew that somehow, someway, all of this would work out for good.

At first the jailers treated Joseph very roughly, but were amazed to see that nothing seemed to shake him. Even during these days—the darkest of his life—Joseph's face had a peace and joy that his heathen captors couldn't understand. But they came to appreciate his attitude. In time, they found it hard to be mean to someone so gentle and courteous. When they unshackled his feet and he could walk again, they found that he was more than willing to help them around the prison. The more freedom they gave him, the more he helped. Soon Joseph was out of the shackles for good. He was still in prison, but the jailer had made him his chief helper. And as time passed, the jailer put more and more trust in Joseph, until he was in charge of the entire prison.

What a change in fortunes this was. Of all the characters in the Bible, Joseph probably had more of an up-and-down roller-coaster life than anyone. You would think, given all the bad things that had happened to him, that Joseph would need years of therapy just to function again. But God was Joseph's counselor. When friendless and alone, Joseph had no one to turn to but God. And God never let him down.

Encouraging other prisoners was one of the things that Joseph did particularly well. Having been through so much himself, he could understand how the other prisoners felt. He encouraged and comforted them, doing what he could to make their lives a little easier until they were released.

Two of the prisoners who remained there a long time had worked for Pharaoh himself. One had been

Pharaoh's chief baker, and the other had been his chief butler. The butler's job was to taste everything Pharaoh was going to eat, to see if anything had been poisoned.

For some reason both the chief baker and the chief butler had fallen out of favor with Pharaoh. And in those days when kings got mad, they didn't play around. They threw the people they were mad at in jail. This is what happened to these two. Then one morning, as Joseph made his rounds in the prison he noticed that both the baker and butler looked sad and worried.

"What's wrong with you two this morning?" he asked. "Are you sick? Has something bad happened?"

"We both had dreams last night" came back the doleful reply. "We are positive that they mean something very important, but we don't know what it could be. There's no one to tell us what they mean, either." If the men had not been in jail they could have asked the wise men of Egypt about the meaning of their dreams. But here they were, locked up, with no idea what the dreams meant.

"God is the one who can tell what dreams mean," Joseph told the baker and butler. "Tell me," he asked them, "what were your dreams?"

"In my dream," said the butler, "I saw a grapevine with three branches. All of a sudden, leaves began to grow on the branches, then blossoms, then grapes. When the grapes were ripe, I picked some and squeezed them into the Pharaoh's cup and brought it to him."

"I have good news," Joseph told the butler.

"The three branches in your dream stand for

three days. In three days Pharaoh will take you out of this cold, dark prison. You will be a free man, and get back your job at the palace."

The butler was thrilled. "The dream makes sense to me now," he told Joseph.

"Could you put in a good word for me when you are back in Pharaoh's house?" Joseph asked him. "See if you can help me get out of prison, because I've done nothing wrong that I should be in here." Of course, the butler promised that he would.

When the baker heard the good meaning of the butler's dream, he was eager to hear what Joseph would say about his dream, too.

"In my dream I was carrying three baskets on my head," said the baker. "In the top basket there were all kinds of tasty baked goods for Pharaoh, and the birds were eating them."

Joseph was stunned. He turned to the baker with a sad and serious look on his face. After all, how do you tell a man that he is about to die? But Joseph knew what he had to do.

"The three baskets stand for three days," he said sadly. "In three days Pharaoh is going to call you to him. But he will not give you back your job as he will do the butler. No, he is going to take your life."

One can only imagine how the baker must have felt at this news. He didn't want to die any more than anyone else would want to. No doubt Joseph spent all the time he could with the baker during the next three days, comforting him and helping him get to know God so that when his time came, he would be ready.

Word about the two dreams and the interpreta-

tion God had given through Joseph spread fast in the prison. "Is he right?" the prisoners wondered. "Can his god really tell the meaning of dreams?"

They didn't have to wait long to find out. Just three days later Pharaoh threw a big birthday party for himself. In the middle of the party he called for the butler and the baker to be brought to him. The butler was forgiven. More than that, he was put back in his old job. But just as Joseph had said, the baker was put to death.

There must have been quite a bit of talk in the prison about the dreams and what had happened to the two men. But somehow, word of the dreams never reached the king. And the butler, whom Joseph had comforted with such good news, was so busy and happy to be back in his old job that he forgot all about him.

As the months passed, Joseph had to give up on the idea that the butler could help make him free. That must have been discouraging, but he never seemed to complain and he didn't give up his faith in God. There he was, doomed to remain in prison for years to come, yet he still trusted God to work everything out somehow.

However, Joseph's time was not wasted. He didn't know it, of course, but he was actually in school. There in prison he saw the results of wickedness and crime. And from this he learned lessons of justice, sympathy, and mercy. Someday—and someday soon—all these lessons would be very much needed, as they would make him a kind and thoughtful ruler.

CHAPTER 21

The King Has Two Dreams

While Pharaoh's butler apparently had forgotten Joseph, God had not forgotten His faithful friend. And when at last the time was right, God Himself sent Pharaoh a couple of dreams.

The dreams were remarkable in that, while they were different, they both seemed to point to the same event. Pharaoh had a fearful suspicion that they meant a great calamity was coming, and he was very anxious to know the truth.

The more Pharaoh thought about the dreams, the more worried he became. He called in his wise men, but they didn't have a clue. As the hours and days went on, the king became more and more agitated, and soon a feeling of terror spread throughout the entire palace.

"What will the king do to us if we don't come up with a reasonable meaning?" the wise men asked each other. Kings in those days were fickle. That means you could be in their good graces one day, and be hanging from a gallows the next. Pharaoh's wise men had every reason to be afraid.

"What does this whole thing mean?" other palace servants asked each other. The king was their leader. If he was worried, they were worried. And then Pharaoh's chief butler remembered something important. Joseph! Feeling guilty about forgetting, he told the king right away.

It was hard for Pharaoh to turn from his wise men and send to the prison for a slave. You know, it would be kind of like Donald Trump going to a homeless person for business advice. But Pharaoh was desperate by then, so he quickly sent for Joseph.

What a change—to go from the dark, damp prison to the palace of the king. While Joseph came as quickly as he could, he had to take care of a few things first. In spite of Joseph's responsible position in helping oversee the prison, it was still a prison. There were no showers, no way to clean up. So before Joseph went to see Pharaoh, he bathed, shaved, and changed from his ragged prison clothes to clean ones provided for him. And that must have felt good after all those years in a dark, smelly prison.

The change between the prison and Pharaoh's palace was even more remarkable. Pharaoh was very rich. His palace was painted in rich colors and was beautifully decorated. At his every word servants jumped to do what he commanded. And he had all the beautiful clothes, finery, and servants that money and power could buy.

As he followed a servant into the palace, Joseph must have looked around in wonder. How bright it all looked after years behind bars. But the riches themselves didn't affect him. He was God's servant, on whatever mission God might send him. He was ready for whatever life might bring.

Joseph's life had been one of high "ups" and deep "downs." He had a loving mother, then suddenly she was gone. He went from a pampered, favored son to the dreary life of a slave. He was head of Potiphar's house, then a prisoner. And now here he was, clean and wearing spotless linen, striding through the luxurious palace corridors on his way to meet the king.

"I dreamed two dreams," Pharaoh began, leaning forward and looking intently at Joseph. "I am sure these dreams mean something bad, very bad. But no one—not even the best of my wise men—can tell me what they mean."

The king looked tired and haggard from loss of sleep, and as Joseph glanced around he saw terror written on every face in the room.

"I can't sleep, I can't rest, until I know what this means." Pharaoh looked Joseph up and down as if trying to figure just what kind of man he was. "I have heard that you can interpret dreams."

If Joseph felt like the pressure was on, he didn't show it. The Bible tells us that God is no respecter of persons. That means that He doesn't treat people any better or worse because of their rank or job. Kings, janitors, army generals, and factory workers are all his children. Joseph knew this, and he wasn't afraid of Pharaoh. Joseph showed Pharaoh the respect due a king, but he wasn't shaking in his sandals or afraid to talk to him.

Pharaoh was king of one of the greatest nations of that time, but Joseph worked for the King of the universe. So while he was humble and polite, the fear of the king's dreams that gripped the whole palace couldn't take hold of Joseph.

"It is not in me to tell the meaning of dreams," Joseph answered the king. "But the God of heaven knows what your dream means."

One can only imagine the tension in the palace at that moment. Surely the word had spread that the king had had the Hebrew prisoner Joseph brought to him. Could he really give the meaning of the king's dreams? Everyone, from the princes and wise men to the lowliest palace maid, just wanted this whole stressful mess to be over.

The king cleared his throat. On the edge of the room the wise men, terrified that they could be put in prison next, leaned in closer. The palace was so quiet you could have heard a beetle scuttle across the floor. Perhaps the queen, who was exhausted herself because the king tossed and turned without sleeping, came in to hear. A servant girl peeked from the doorway, and even God and the angels in heaven were watching as Pharaoh told the story of his dreams, his frightening dreams.

CHAPTER 22

The King Tells His Dreams

I was standing by the banks of the Nile River," Pharaoh began. "While I was there, seven cows came and stood among the reeds of the riverbank. They were very fat and sassy. It seemed to me as though they hadn't missed a meal in their entire lives. They were the best-looking cows I've ever seen in all the land of Egypt."

Joseph listened carefully. He was deep in thought and prayer as the king went on.

"While the seven good-looking cows stood there, another seven cows came up by the riverbank. The second seven were the worst-looking cows I've ever seen. Their ribs stuck out, and they had a wild look in their eyes. Their legs were wobbly, and their bodies were skin and bones."

Joseph nodded politely as the king continued with his story.

"I was wishing that those seven bad-looking cows would go away, never to be seen again, when a horrible thing happened! The seven skinny cows attacked the seven fat cows, gobbling them right down. And what was worse, after eating the fat cows the seven skinny cows were just as thin as they were before! In fact, they looked even worse to me."

The king's face puckered, and the listening people shuddered at the thought. Joseph solemnly nodded, and the king plunged on once again.

"If that wasn't bad enough, another dream soon followed. I saw seven ears of corn, so full and fat and delicious that if I had been awake I would have eaten them for sure. But while I watched, another stalk grew up. It too had seven ears, but these were thin and withered, burned by the east wind."

"Ohhhhh," gasped a little servant girl who peered at the king from behind a pillar. The child's mother, whose job was to fan the king, gave her a scolding look that shushed her up very quickly.

The king hadn't noticed, for he was reliving his dream. "Then the withered, skinny ears of corn ate the full, fat ears! And what is worse, after eating them the skinny ears looked as bad as before." He raised a trembling hand. "I fear that something bad, very bad, is about to happen. What does your god tell you about my dream?"

Joseph didn't hesitate. "My God did send these dreams to tell you what will happen in Egypt. You had two dreams, but they both mean the same thing.

"The seven fat cows and the seven fat ears of corn stand for seven years of plenty. There will be wonderful harvests during those years, like the land of Egypt has never seen before."

Pharaoh nodded. "Yes, yes. And then?"

"The seven skinny cows and the seven skinny ears of corn stand for seven years of famine. After the seven years of plenty are over, there will be seven years of famine. The seven years of famine will be so terrible that your people will almost forget the seven years of plenty.

"You must get ready," Joseph told the king. "You must find a capable man to be in charge of gathering lots of food. You will need to build huge storehouses in which to put all the food. It will be a big job, and take a lot of organization. Every year of plenty, take a fifth of all the harvest of the land of Egypt and put it in storage barns. That way you can save ahead for the famine, and no one will starve."

The king looked relieved. Even though something very bad was about to happen to his country, Joseph's God was giving him time to get ready for it.

"Thank you, Joseph," the king said. "I want to talk this over with my wise men."

The Bible doesn't tell us how much time passed as the king and his wise men talked things over. It surely took at least a few days for the king to digest everything Joseph had told him, and work with his advisors, his wise men, to decide what he should do next. They must have talked about how much it would cost to build large buildings to hold the grain that needed to be stored. They probably went over a list of men who could supervise all the people they'd need to get this done.

During this time Joseph must have wondered what his own fate would be. But he had learned long ago to trust in God to guide him day by day. His life was in God's hands, and he knew that somehow, in the end, everything would work out.

CHAPTER 23

From the Dungeon to the Throne

Joseph!"

Once again Joseph found himself called to stand before Pharaoh.

Once again he was ushered through the luxurious hallways of the palace, past the scurrying servants and pondering, portly wise men. Servants busily fanned the king—lest a pesky fly should land on his royal arm—and the whole palace jumped at the snap of his finger.

"My wise men and I have considered the dream and what it means," the king broke into Joseph's thoughts. "The interpretation your God gave you makes sense. We have been given seven years to get ready for the worst famine ever. We all agree that we need someone very wise and very capable. We need a man who has the spirit of your god to take on this important job."

Pharaoh's eyes rested on the handsome young man standing before him. "There is only one person in my kingdom like that, Joseph. I am placing you over my entire house and my entire kingdom. In all the land of Egypt, only I will be greater than you."

Joseph bowed politely to the king. But though he was calm on the outside, inside his heart was racing. He would not return to prison. He was going from the prison to the palace, from the dungeon to a throne.

Pharaoh's chief butler stood in the background with a very pleased look on his face. Stung with guilt over forgetting Joseph when his own dream had been interpreted, he had gone out of his way to tell Pharaoh what a capable man Joseph was, and how everything he touched, God blessed.

Pharaoh had done his homework. We don't know if he ever talked to Potiphar or if Potiphar was even around at that point. But Pharaoh was sure of one thing: Joseph was the man for the job. And he lost no time in putting his plan into action.

"Here is my ring." With some effort Pharaoh slipped it off his finger. The head of the ring was inscribed with the king's name. Stamped in clay or wax, it gave Joseph the authority to act for the king. "My servants are getting one of my Ferrari chariots with the team of horses that won the Pyramid Derby ready for you even as we speak."

He didn't give Joseph a chance to reply, but continued giving instructions. "You have an appointment with my tailor tomorrow. You must have clothes worthy of your position as prime minister of Egypt. And of course there will be a ceremony installing you in your new position.

All of my counselors, wise men, and servants are at your command, as are the contractors and builders. You will be given maps of Egypt and the population of each city and each section of the country. Come up with a plan to build all the storehouses you need. All the workers and materials you ask for will be provided."

For just an instant Joseph let himself lean against a table. His head was spinning. He could hardly keep up with the king's directions.

"I have an office set up for you over the palace gardens," Pharaoh went on. "Of course, you will be traveling a lot to oversee the planning and building and later, the harvesting and collecting of grain. But you can direct things from your office as well. Meet with me often and let me know how things go.

"You will also have a new name: Zaphenath-Panea."

Joseph blinked. OK. That would take getting used to.

"Let's see. Is there anything else?"

For someone who had become used to huge, sudden changes in his life, Joseph looked stunned. Throughout the trials and troubles of the past 13 years he had held to the belief that God had a purpose for his life. And now he knew the reason God had let him be sold and brought to Egypt. He didn't fully understand, but he could begin to see the reason.

"Oh yes, one more thing. The prime minister of Egypt must be a married man. My chief wise man has chosen a young woman for you. She is the daughter of the high priest to our god On, and she is very beautiful."

At last Pharaoh paused and gave a nod and smile at his new assistant. "Do you have any questions?"

"No, Your Highness. I mean, yes, I do! But I'm afraid I don't know what they are." Even the organized and capable Joseph reeled with the size and magnitude of the job and the changes ahead of him. His life had come full circle in a hurry.

"Very well, then. If you need anything, let me or one of my assistants know. I am told that whatever you touch, your god blesses. I know you will do a good job."

"Yes, Your Highness!"

One of the king's assistants handed Joseph a piece of papyrus with all his appointments written down on it. With his personal planner tucked under his arm, Joseph headed out to the chariot, where the fastest horses in the kingdom were prancing and ready to run. So much to do in so little time! There were clothes to have fitted, an office to settle into, a home to get used to, a wife to meet, and most of all, a large kingdom to prepare for a deadly famine. But with God's help, Joseph was up to it.

Whatever God gave him to do, whether cleaning the prison toilets or building barns for Pharaoh, Joseph gave it everything he had. He was God's minuteman, ready, willing, and able to meet his greatest assignment ever.

CHAPTER 24

Prime Minister of Egypt

The next few days, then weeks and years, were very busy ones for Joseph. They were happy years, too. Being prime minister of Egypt was an astonishing honor. He had power, prestige, money, respect, and work that he enjoyed. He had good looks, a beautiful wife, and two baby boys. Next to the king, Joseph was the most important man in the kingdom. He had everything he could want or ask for—except the joy of seeing or hearing from his father again.

Joseph had a lot of responsibility in his new job. The land of Egypt was very large, with a number of cities and hundreds of thousands of people. Joseph didn't have a cell phone, a jet plane, or even an electric drill. Yet he had to plan and oversee the building of many storehouses, plus the collecting and storing of one fifth of all the food Egypt grew every year for seven years. And what a lot of food there was! When God said seven years of plenty, He meant seven years of plenty.

Remember that the fat cows and the fat ears of corn Pharaoh saw in his dream were unlike anything Egypt had seen before. It may have been tempting for some people to wonder if going to all that trouble and expense was really worth it. It was an act of faith in God, on the part of both Pharaoh and Joseph, to store up all that grain based on two little dreams. But the dreams had impressed and frightened him so much that Pharaoh never questioned the wisdom of it all. And Joseph moved forward full speed to protect the land of Egypt from the terrible famine that was soon to come.

And then came the eighth year. The entire land of Egypt watched to see if God's word would come true. The first half of the king's dreams had certainly been fulfilled. Never before could anyone remember such good harvests. Some people had stored up grain for themselves so they wouldn't have to buy from Pharaoh during the coming famine, at least not for a while.

And sure enough, the yearly flooding of the Nile, caused by rains in faraway Ethiopia, did not come. Without the flooding, the land remained dry. And so in the eighth year after the dreams there was no planting and no grain to harvest. When the famine hit, it was everything God had predicted and more.

Soon the people of Egypt ran out of food in their

cupboards and wherever else they had stored it. They came to Joseph, and he was ready for them, of course. Opening up the storehouses of grain, he started selling by the bushel and wagonload.

All the God-given wisdom Joseph showed in storing up the grain he now used in doling it out. The world has always had greedy people who would want more than their share during times of trouble. There were other nations to think about too—many of whom were soon beating a path straight to Joseph and Pharaoh's door. Years before, Joseph had tried to figure out how much would be needed to feed all of Egypt and people from other starving countries during the seven years of famine. Now care had to be taken in knowing how much to sell.

Far away from Egypt the famine affected Jacob's family too. The grass was brown and dry. The sheep and goats grew thin. But somehow for the first couple of years there was always food on the table for the 11 brothers, their wives and children, and for the servants and others that lived in Jacob's camp. But eventually supplies got so low that they dared not go on without finding somewhere they could buy food. Things were getting desperate.

"I heard they have grain for sale in Egypt," Jacob told his sons. He'd been talking to someone from a passing caravan. "I want you to go see if you can buy us some corn or grain."

Jacob's sons were glad to do it. Actually, they didn't have a lot of options. Their families and servants were starting to get hungry. Their wives were already rationing the food, and they had felt some low growls in their own stomachs.

"Leave Benjamin with me," Jacob told them. "I already lost Joseph. I don't want to lose Benjamin, too."

They didn't have a problem with that. Though more than 20 years had passed, Jacob had never stopped grieving for Joseph. They didn't want to go through that again, so they were glad to leave their youngest brother behind. They packed up their donkeys and were on their way. The trip must have been a little scary. They were tough men, but robbers and ruffians traveled the rugged roads leading toward Egypt. No doubt Jacob raised his hands and gave a very special prayer for them before they headed out on their long and treacherous trip. And then they were gone, waving one last time as they headed hopefully over the horizon.

CHAPTER 25

The Dreamer's Dream Comes True

As busy as Joseph was, it's hard to imagine that he personally saw everyone who wanted to buy food in the land of Egypt. He probably had many helpers, each working at storehouses around the country, to get the food out to the people. There may have been limits, however, to how much food the Egyptians would sell to foreigners. Or maybe Joseph had heard that the famine had hit the land of Canaan, also, and he was waiting and hoping that his brothers would come. Perhaps this is why, before they could buy grain, Joseph's brothers had to visit the prime minister of Egypt.

Many years had gone by now since Joseph

had been sold into slavery at age 17. He had been about 30 when he had interpreted Pharaoh's dreams. The seven years of plenty had already passed by, and the famine was well under way. So it had been at least 20 years since Joseph had last seen his brothers. And then it happened. His 10 older brothers filed into his audience room. And they all bowed down to him just as he'd seen in his dreams.

Joseph sat on a platform in front of them. He was wearing the same shoulder-length black wig as other Egyptians officials wore and the clothes of a nobleman. His brothers didn't recognize him, of course. He was 20 years older than the last time they'd seen him, and he was good at masking how he felt. Nothing at all clued them as to who he was.

"What are you here for?" he asked roughly in the Egyptian language. An interpreter translated his words into Hebrew and Joseph's brothers' replies into Egyptian.

"We came here to buy grain for our families so they won't go hungry," they replied.

Joseph stared at them sternly. His eyes went from one to the other until they began to feel uncomfortable. After all these years, the prime minister of Egypt had some major questions about these brothers of his. If he had lived today, some would think Joseph would have needed years of therapy to recover from the emotional wounds of his childhood. But God was Joseph's therapist. He had given Joseph not only healing, but a wise and understanding heart.

It only took an instant to see that Benjamin was missing. He wondered if they had tried to finish him off too. He wanted to ask about Benjamin and about his father, but he didn't trust them to tell the truth. So he decided to test them and see what he could learn without telling them who he was.

"You are spies," he told them as if he were angry. "You came to spy out the land, and take word back to our enemies."

"Oh no, we are not spies," they protested. "We are all brothers. Our father had 12 sons. One is dead. One is with his father, and we 10 are here."

"Well, why don't you prove it?" Joseph shot back. "I'll keep nine of you here in my prison. One of you can go back and get your brother. When I see him, I'll know you are telling the truth, and then I'll sell you some food."

"Our father is grieving already over the loss of his son," they told him. "He will never let the youngest son come here. If you put nine of us in jail, we will never get out."

Joseph stood up. "Throw them in jail," he ordered his guards, and strode from the room.

CHAPTER • 26

The Brothers
Try Out the Jail

The three days spent in jail were a great time of soul-searching for Joseph's 10 brothers. They felt they were being punished because of their sin. They had sinned against their brother, against their father, and most of all, against God. They had watched the terrible grief of their father when Joseph was gone, but had never relented and told him the truth. And their guilt— their terrible guilt—had followed them all of those years. They had thought they would be happy when Joseph was gone, but instead they had felt nothing but sadness.

Joseph didn't want to leave his brothers in jail too long. He knew they needed to return home. Already their families and his father could be starving.

He didn't really want them in jail. He just wanted to see what sort of men they had become. So after three days he had them brought before him again.

"I will keep one of you here in my jail," he told them. "The rest of you may buy food and take it back to your families. But bring your other brother back to show me you are telling the truth. Unless you bring him to me, you'll never get any more food, and the one sitting in jail will never get out."

At that the brothers all talked at once. They didn't know that Joseph understood every word. "This is happening to us because of what we did to Joseph," one said. "We are being punished because when he cried for his life, we wouldn't listen!"

"Didn't I tell you not to hurt the child?" Reuben scolded. "But no, you had to have your way. God has seen our guilt, and now we will pay."

"Take that one, right there." Joseph pointed to Simeon. It had been Simeon's idea to sell Joseph as a slave. Simeon had been the meanest, the cruelest, and in many ways the worst of the bunch. When Joseph had cried to his brothers and pleaded for his life, some of them would have relented. But Simeon talked them into sticking with their plan. Joseph had forgiven Simeon long ago, but he had never forgotten who the ringleader was.

Quickly Simeon's hands were tied behind his back, and he was marched out of the room.

"Goodbye," his brothers sadly called after him. Then he was gone, perhaps to the same prison where Joseph had spent several years of his life. Then

The Brothers Try Out the Jail

Joseph dismissed the others, sternly reminding them not to return without the youngest son.

They went and bought as much grain as their donkeys could carry, and started the long trip home. It was not a happy journey. All the way they talked about breaking the news to their father that Simeon had been kept in an Egyptian jail. And how would they ever tell Jacob that they dared not return to Egypt without Benjamin?

There was joy, great joy, in Jacob's camp when the little procession finally rounded the last bend and came into view. Here was food, wonderful food! And how good it was to see everyone again! But it didn't take Jacob long to figure out that someone was missing. Perhaps he even counted them off on his fingers!

"Where is Simeon?" Jacob asked, a worried look on his face.

"Where is our daddy?" Simeon's children cried.

"Where is my husband?" asked Simeon's wife.

"Ummm . . ." Reuben cleared his throat. "We ran into a bit of trouble in Egypt." Then he told the whole family about their difficulty with the prime minister. He told them about the three days they'd spent in jail and the Egyptian's demand that their youngest brother come back with them or they'd get no more grain from Egypt.

Jacob was devastated. He had already lost one son. And Simeon was in prison in a foreign land. He would never let Benjamin go. He covered his face with his hands. "My son shall not go down with you," he said. "His brother is dead, and he is the only one left."

And that was that, until they all got hungry again.

CHAPTER 27

Benjamin Takes a Trip

Jacob's sons knew better than to talk to their father about sending Benjamin on the next trip to Egypt. They knew how strongly Jacob felt about letting Benjamin go. There was no use even to ask.

But as the weeks turned into months and the famine wore on, it became increasingly clear that they must make another trip to Egypt for food. There was also the problem of Simeon, who was wasting away in the depths of an Egyptian jail. The day finally came when Jacob called his sons to him. "Go back down to Egypt and buy us a little food," he said. There was a long pause before Judah stepped up and said exactly what everyone knew needed to be said.

"The man in Egypt strictly told us not to bother coming unless our brother was with us," he said.

Jacob sighed. As the days had gone by, his mind had adjusted to the truth. Benjamin would have to go.

"Joseph is gone, and Simeon is gone," he said and his voice trembled. "Now soon Benjamin will be gone too. If I must suffer this loss, then I must."

"I will see to it that Benjamin comes back safely," Judah promised. "You can hold me responsible if anything happens to him. I give you my word that I will take care of him."

Soon the donkeys were saddled and the brothers were on their way. They took extra money this time, since something strange had happened at the end of their last trip. When they had opened their bags full of grain, each brother had found money in the top of his bag! And it was the exact amount of money that they had paid for the grain.

No doubt they had a strange feeling as their steps took them closer and closer to Egypt. They needed to make this trip, but every fiber in their bodies wanted to run the other direction. They were desperate for more food and they wanted to rescue Simeon, but the last person they wanted to see was the prime minister. It wasn't long, however, before they arrived and stood before Joseph. When he saw that Benjamin was with them, he told his assistant to take them all to his house. "Have the cook prepare dinner for us," he said. "I will eat with them at noon."

Joseph's brothers didn't understand the conversation, of course, and were frightened when told they were being taken to the prime minister's house. "It's because of the silver that we found in our sacks," they told each other. "We are going to be captured and put in prison."

So they went to the assistant and told him about the money they'd found in their bags on their way back home from their first visit.

"Peace be to you," the man told them. "Do not be afraid. I have the money you paid. The God of your father must have put money back in your sacks."

There were nine sighs of relief as the brothers realized they wouldn't be in trouble over the money. They were even happier when Simeon came into the room.

Soon they were ushered into the prime minister's house. They were given water so they could wash their hands and dusty feet. Then they waited for the prime minister to arrive. It didn't take long.

"We brought our brother as you requested," Judah told the ruler, "and we also brought you some gifts." Then all 11 of Joseph's brothers, including Benjamin, bowed down to him. This was the custom of the day because Joseph was the ruler, but it was also the fulfillment of the dream Joseph had had so many years ago.

"Hello," Joseph said to them, and his tone was much friendlier than before. Then he couldn't wait to ask the most important question of all. "Is your father well, the old man you spoke about? Is he still alive?"

"Our father is still alive and in good health," the brothers replied. And once again they knelt then bowed with their faces to the floor. They stood, and Joseph's eyes rested on Benjamin. "Is this the younger brother you told me about?" he asked.

"Yes" came back the reply.

Tears filled Joseph's eyes. "May God bless you, my son."

Joseph had held up very well so far, but now his voice cracked with emotion. Quickly he turned away, going to a side room where he could weep in private. After a while, when Joseph felt he could go on, he washed his face, wiped his eyes, and went back to his brothers again. He had invited them to be his guests at a dinner, and his servants had everything ready.

"Isn't it strange that we're seated in order of our ages?" the brothers wondered to each other. "How does he know which one of us is the oldest?"

But stranger things were still to come. Joseph was testing his brothers—testing to see if they hated Benjamin the way they hated him, testing to see if his brothers really had changed. The next test came when Benjamin received five times more food than anyone else. Joseph, who sat at a separate table because of the custom of the Egyptians, listened closely to see what was said. His brothers still didn't know that he understood their every word, so they felt free to say what they really thought. And Joseph was pleased to see that no one seemed to mind that Benjamin had been honored by having more food than the rest.

The final test—and the hardest one for the brothers—came after they'd bought more grain and were on their way home. It began when Joseph told his servant to place his silver cup in the top of Benjamin's sack. This was a very special cup. The Egyptians thought it had the power to tell if someone put poison in whatever drink it held.

Benjamin Takes a Trip

Joseph's brothers had no idea that the prime minister's cup was in one of their bags. They were too busy being thrilled that Simeon was free, overjoyed that Benjamin was still with them, and happy to be taking food back to their hungry families in Canaan. So once again they started out on their journey, with no idea that the biggest trouble of all lay just ahead.

CHAPTER 28

"You Stole My Cup!"

Jacob's 11 sons had scarcely reached the outskirts of the Egyptian city when they heard the thunder of hoof-beats behind them. "Look at those clouds of dust," they said to each other. They didn't see any reason to run, as they hadn't done anything wrong. They couldn't have gotten away if they'd wanted to, not on donkeys loaded with bags of food.

Joseph's head servant wheeled his stallion up to the brothers and glared down at them. "What have you done?" he demanded

"What do you mean, what have we done?" They were puzzled, but still thought it was a mistake.

"Why have

you repaid good with evil?" he asked. "The prime minister treated you well. He served dinner to you in his house. He let your brother out of prison and sold you the food you needed. And what did you do? Stole his silver cup, that's what!"

"How can you say that?" The brothers were respectful but shocked. "God forbid that we would ever do anything like that. When we found extra money in our sacks, didn't we bring it back to you? Why would we then try to steal from your master? If you find the cup with any of us, that man will die and the rest of us will be your servants for the rest of our lives."

"That's exactly what we will do," replied the Egyptian, though he changed it to a lesser punishment. "The man who has the cup will be my servant. The rest of you may go free."

The men stood back while the Egyptian guards searched their bags of grain and other food. Somehow even these Egyptians seemed to know the birth order of the brothers. Once again they started at the oldest and worked their way down to the youngest.

And then . . .

"Here it is!" The guard held the cup—the shining, ornate silver cup—high over his head. He had found it in Benjamin's sack! A great, anguished groan rose up from the other men. They were as shocked and sad as if Benjamin had just died. Grabbing their own robes, they ripped them in agony. This was a sign of great grief and usually done only at a funeral or other very sad occasion.

They turned their donkeys around. Slowly they mounted and, trembling from head to foot, rode be-

hind the servant back to the palace. Joseph was still there, standing tall and stern in all the finery of his high office. The men fell on their faces before him.

"I can't believe what you did!" Joseph raged. "Don't you think I am smart enough to figure things out?"

"What can I say to my lord?" Judah stepped forward. "How can we clear ourselves? God is punishing us for our sins, and now we will be your servants—both we and the one whom you found with the cup."

The brothers couldn't bear the thought of facing their father without Benjamin. They would actually rather stay and be slaves with their brother than return home without him. What a change this was from how they had felt about Joseph.

"I wouldn't even think of having you all as my slaves" came back the reply. "The man who had the cup—he will be my servant. The rest of you may go free."

At this Judah was nearly overcome with grief. Yet he knew he had to keep talking. Somehow, with God's help, he must save Benjamin. "O my lord," Judah said, stepping a little closer to Joseph. "Please let me say something to you, and I beg you not to be angry."

Then, in words that only a loving brother could use, Judah told the story of how Joseph had been lost and their father's heart had been broken. He told Joseph how Benjamin was the only son of Rachel, whom Jacob had dearly loved, left. He told how Jacob had not wanted Benjamin to travel to Egypt, and how he himself had promised to bring Benjamin safely back.

Again Judah fell on his knees before Joseph. "I cannot bear to see the grief of my father if I don't bring Benjamin back. Please, oh, please, let me stay in Egypt in his place. I will stay here and be your servant, only let Benjamin go back to our father."

Joseph had seen enough. He knew now that his brothers, who had once been so hateful and cruel, had truly changed. Joseph's tests for his brothers were over, and the brothers had passed with flying colors.

Joseph turned to the captain of his guard and his other attendants. "Everyone leave the room!" he commanded in Egyptian. His guards and other officials may have been surprised or even worried about leaving him alone with these men, but they quickly obeyed.

Then the prime minister of Egypt reached down to take Judah's hand and lift him to his feet. "I am Joseph," he said in Hebrew. "Is my father really alive?"

Joseph's brothers were shocked and too scared to reply. The prime minister of Egypt neither looked nor acted anything liked the teenage boy they had sold into slavery so many years before. And the memory of what they'd done to him was all too vivid in their minds. Joseph saw the fear on their faces and hurried to set them at ease.

"Come close to me," he said. "Don't be afraid of me." He waited, tears streaming down his face as slowly his brothers crept toward him.

"My brothers, don't be angry with yourselves that you sold me into Egypt," he told them. "It was God who sent me here to save the lives of many people from this famine."

Then Joseph told his brothers that the famine would last another five years. "I am sending you

home with wagons to bring everybody back," he told them. "I will give you a place to stay and plenty of food here in the land of Egypt. And I want to see my father again."

Joseph threw his arms around Benjamin and wept so loudly that everyone in the palace heard him. Then going from brother to brother, he kissed each one and wept over them as each begged his forgiveness.

"I already have forgiven you," Joseph told them. "I did it long ago." If he had allowed himself to wallow in bitterness, he could never have had the success in life that he had.

Joseph talked with his brothers for a long while, for they certainly had a lot of news to catch up on. Then he got together wagons and lots of food to send to his family in Canaan.

When Pharaoh heard that Joseph's family had come, he and his officials were pleased. He told Joseph, "Tell your brothers to load up their families and their animals and come to Egypt. I will give them some of the best land we have." So it was that 11 brothers were soon on their way back to Canaan, loaded down with good things from Joseph and good news for their father about the son he had lost so many years before.

CHAPTER 29

Moving to Egypt

They're coming! Our fathers are coming!" Children raced through Jacob's camp shouting to anyone within earshot. Now there'd be good things to eat, and Grandfather Jacob would be happy again.

Jacob was on his feet, his hand shading his eyes as he looked into the distance. Sure enough, he saw a caravan coming in the distance. But where were the donkeys? His sons had left riding on donkeys. Now wagons were coming and carts and many more donkeys, all laden with bags of food.

But where was Benjamin. Had his son returned? He wanted to see Benjamin!

Excited, the children ran to meet the wagons and their fathers. Before long they were running back as fast as they could. "Uncle Benjamin is here! Uncle Simeon is here!" And Jacob leaned on his staff with tears running down his cheeks and into his long gray beard.

Benjamin *was* back. Now he was hugging his father, kissing him on both cheeks. But what was this? Where did the wagons come from? Why all the extra donkeys?

By now the wives and servants had joined the crowd. Everyone wanted to welcome the travelers and to see what they had brought. The whole camp broke into noisy rejoicing, little knowing that the best was yet to come.

"Oh, I am so happy you are all here and safe," Jacob said. He went from son to son, hugging each one and kissing both cheeks. But now he was exhausted from the excitement. He sank on to a bench and looked his sons over from head to toe. Something seemed different about them, but he wasn't sure what. They *looked* different. They looked happier, but it was something else. They looked worried, too.

Quickly the servants began unloading the animals. Women stirred up the cooking fires and grabbed their daughters to help them prepare food. Jacob called Simeon to him, wanting to know how he'd been treated in prison. And he wouldn't let Benjamin out of his sight. "My son, my son," he repeated, holding the young man's face in his hands.

"Father, we have some news for you," Reuben, the oldest son, said. "We need to talk. Let's go to your tent."

"What is it, my sons?" Suddenly Jacob felt frightened. There was something in Reuben's voice that warned him this was not good.

Reuben took his arm. "No. Don't be afraid. But we should talk—all of us—with you alone."

With the men seated on pillows and rugs Reuben started the terrible story. "It was many years ago . . ." he began, then stopped.

"We did something very wrong," Judah slowly added. "It was a very great sin, and it has haunted us all this time."

"But what?" Jacob's voice was shrill. "What?"

Levi twisted his hands together. "We must confess to you, Father."

Simeon's voice shook. "We are so sorry we hurt you."

Jacob half stood, then sank back down. His hands trembled on his staff. "I don't understand. How did you hurt me?"

Then his sons began talking at once. "Here is the good news, Father. Joseph is still alive. He is the ruler of Egypt. He's next to the pharaoh. The bad news, Father"—and here Judah's voice broke—"is that Joseph would never have been gone in the first place if it wasn't for our sin."

Jacob shook from head to foot and Benjamin hurried over to sit next to him.

"What are you saying?" Jacob demanded. "Why do you lie to an old man?"

"Will you forgive us, Father?"

"Forgive us."

"Forgive us . . ."

And so Jacob's sons told him how they'd seen

Joseph coming to the grassland in Dothan that day so long ago. That they'd thrown him in a pit, then sold him into slavery. One by one, each man confessed his own part in the crime. Jacob was so overwhelmed that he almost passed out. Never had he suspected that his sons could do something this low. But the agony of that realization was quickly overshadowed by the ecstasy of the very idea that Joseph—his beloved and long-missing Joseph—was still alive!

"I forgive you, my sons," Jacob told them. "I forgive you."

Jacob, of all men, knew what it was to be plagued by guilt. Now he knew what had bothered his sons for so many years. He understood that his favoritism toward Joseph had helped the brothers to hate him, and he was sorry for that. And he saw how God had worked through this terrible situation to bring things together in the end. Joseph was still alive! His son was prime minister over all the land of Egypt. And best of all, he could see Joseph again before he died.

CHAPTER 30

Reunited at Last!

Sometimes when parents think they have lost a child the worst really has happened. They never see that child again. This is what happened when Jacob left his mother to flee Esau. Both he and Rebekah had hoped that after Esau simmered down a bit Jacob could come home. But it didn't work out that way. Jacob had spent 20 years working for Laban, and by the time he did come home, his mother was dead. She had passed to her rest during the years he was away. This was a real heartbreak for Jacob, for even though he was around 90 at the time, he loved his mother very much. And back then, being 90 was not the same as it is today. As the story of Jacob wrestling with Jesus shows us, at 90 he was still a very strong man.

Of course, Jacob believed that Joseph had been killed by wild animals. He had his blood-soaked robe to prove it. Thinking him dead, he'd never dreamed that he'd see him again. However, God had other plans.

As happy as Jacob was about being reunited with Joseph, he was worried about moving to Egypt. Jacob knew about the prophecy made to Abraham that someday his children would be slaves in a foreign land. And Jacob was an old man by this time. Surely it was hard for him to leave the land of Canaan where he had lived so long.

At the town of Beersheba Jacob stopped the long caravan. He wanted to make a thank offering to God and to ask for reassurance that God would be with them in Egypt. That night God came to him in a dream. "Don't be afraid," a voice boomed in the darkness. Jacob had fallen asleep worrying about the move and God sent an angel to strengthen his faith. "While your children are in Egypt, I will make them into a great nation.

"You will see Joseph again," the angel went on. "In fact, he will even be with you when you die."

God knew that the land of Canaan was not a good place to grow a nation of His people. The heathen tribes there were warlike and very strong. If he had blessed Abraham, Isaac, or Jacob with hundreds of grandchildren, there wouldn't have been room enough in the land for them to stay together. If they had fanned out into the heathen tribes, they would have been tempted to mix with the heathen and start living as they did.

God didn't want Jacob's children to fight with the Canaanites for land either. It was too soon. God was still giving the Canaanites time to turn back to Him. God is very patient. He does not want to see anyone suffer. The same God who was the God of Abraham, Isaac, and Jacob wanted to be the God of the Canaanites. And being the fair God that He is, He gave them many years to respond to His love.

Jacob was comforted by the angel's message. He knew that God would be with him, that he would see Joseph again, and that God had a plan for everything happening in his life.

Meanwhile, in Egypt, Joseph was watching and waiting. He had his helpers on the lookout, too, to let him know when the caravan from Canaan grew close to Egypt. And when, at last, Joseph heard that his father was nearby, he didn't wait another minute. Hopping into his chariot, he raced his horses at full speed to meet his father.

In his hurry to see Jacob, Joseph forgot that he was the prime minister of Egypt. He forgot that normally he was dignified and careful. He hardly noticed that an entire entourage of Egyptian servants and soldiers had leaped on their horses and in their chariots and were riding with him, for the prime minister must be attended at all times. None of that mattered at this moment. There was his daddy—the one he had missed and wanted to see for so long! Joseph was so happy he leaped out of his chariot and raced into Jacob's waiting arms. They hugged and wept on each other's necks for what the Bible says was "a good while" (Genesis 46:29, KJV).

There was so much to talk about, so much to say, so many years to catch up on. What a happy time that was for Jacob and Joseph. And their entire family—not to mention the whole land of Egypt—was happy with them.

Joseph took five of his brothers to see the king, who officially gave the family land in Goshen where they could live and raise their flocks. Pharaoh liked Joseph so well that he might have offered the brothers jobs in his kingdom, but Joseph was against this. He knew the temptations of the royal palace, and that God had called Israel's family to be separate. So he coached his brothers on what to say to Pharaoh so he would let them settle in the country.

Then Joseph brought his father to the royal palace and presented him to Pharaoh.

We can imagine Pharaoh in his crisp, white linen robe sitting in an ornate chair, a wide gold collar around his neck and laying on his shoulders. He looked at the bent and weathered man before him and at the pride in the eyes of the old man's son.

"How old are you?" the king asked Jacob.

"The years of my journey have been one hundred and thirty," he replied. And Jacob, who had lived all his life in tents of woven wool and goat hair, lifted his hand and pronounced on Pharaoh a blessing from the living God.

• • •

By now Jacob was quite an old man. When he learned that Joseph was alive he had said, "If I can just see him, then I can pass to my rest in peace."

But God had other plans. He blessed Jacob with 17 more years in Egypt, and they were some of the happiest years of his life. Jacob's life had held a lot of trouble. There was the lie he had told his father that forced him to flee from Esau. There was the lie that Laban and Leah had forced on him, and the resulting bickering and jealousy in his home. There was the pain and shame of the sins of his sons—killing all the men of Shechem and selling their own brother into slavery. But things were different now.

Jacob could see that his sons had truly changed. Gone was the bitterness and fighting. They had wholeheartedly given their lives to God. Jacob could also see that the land of Egypt was a great place for God to grow His nation. The Egyptians looked on shepherds with disgust, so there wasn't much chance of Jacob's family mingling with them. And in the land of Goshen there was plenty of room, and peace, to grow large families and teach them about God.

Best of all, here in Egypt was Joseph, who spent every moment he could with his aging father. In Joseph's early years, Jacob showered all the love and care that he could on Joseph. Now Joseph was able to return that love. As prime minister of Egypt, Joseph was a wealthy man, and he made certain that his father and his entire family were very well taken care of.

So the last years of Jacob's life passed peacefully. It was a fitting and happy ending for a man who'd often struggled with sorrow and loss. As time passed and Jacob became more and more frail, he realized that he was close to death. Just as Abraham and Isaac before him, Jacob wanted to pass the blessings of God on to his sons. So he called them together, to be around his bedside, one last time.

CHAPTER 31

Splitting the Birthright

It must have been a solemn occasion when Jacob's family gathered around his bed that day. Nobody wanted to say goodbye, yet all knew that the time had come. As a young man, Jacob had wanted the birthright more than anything else in the world. Though he had traveled a difficult road, he now had the birthright. More than that, he had the assurance that the God who had watched over him for 147 years would be with him during these, the last moments of his life.

Many times before, Jacob had prayed for the future of his sons and family. And now as he was about to give his final blessing, the Holy Spirit came into him in an even deeper way, showing him many things about their future.

"Reuben, you were my first baby boy," Jacob began. "You were the beginning of my strength, power, and dignity. But you are as unstable as the waves of the sea. You are not going to do very well."

These words must have been hard for Reuben to hear, yet he deserved them. Though Reuben had been against his brothers harming Joseph, he had not had the courage to stop them from throwing him into a pit to die. It was while he was away that Joseph was sold to the Ishmaelites. And earlier on in his life he had broken the seventh commandment. He had spent a night with one of his father's wives, as if she were his wife. Jacob's words about Reuben did come true. Reuben never was much of a leader. The tribe of Reuben was always a small and unimportant one. It was also one of the first tribes taken captive when the nation of Israel sinned.

"Simeon and Levi, your children will be scattered in Israel," Jacob went on. Simeon and Levi had led out in the murder of the men of Shechem. They had also been the leaders in selling Joseph.

True to the prophecy of Jacob, the tribe of Simeon grew small and was swallowed up by the other tribes in Israel. Levi was scattered all over Israel, too, but that scattering became a blessing. Levi must have been very sorry for his sin and became a godly man, for his children were some of the only ones who stood for right during the time of Moses. Because of this stand for right God blessed the Levites by making them the priests of the nation. So even though Levi had done wrong and at first got what seemed like a curse, that curse later became a blessing.

"Judah, you are the one your brothers will say good things about," Jacob went on. "Your hand will be on the neck of your enemies, and your father's children will bow down before you. You will be as strong as a lion and a line of kings will be in your tribe. One day the greatest king of all—the Messiah—will be born into your family, and all the people will gather around Him."

Although Jacob said something about each of the other brothers, his finest words were about Joseph.

"Joseph, you were like a branch of a tree, loaded with fruit," Jacob said. "There were those who hated you, who shot arrows at you, and they hurt you very badly. But you trusted in God, and He made you very strong. God will bless you, and you will be very blessed, because you took a stand and acted differently from your brothers."

Gone were the days of jealousy, bickering, and backbiting among the brothers. In spite of their faults, they had matured into men who really loved God and wanted to do His will. Jacob could give Joseph a special blessing—and even divide up the birthright—in peace.

The spiritual part of the birthright eventually went to Levi, when his children became the priests of Israel. Leadership and the promise of the Messiah went to Judah, and the double part of Jacob's money went to Joseph.

Jacob was not trying to show favorites when he gave the brothers his final blessing. He had forgiven them all, and he loved them to his last breath. He was very kind and tender, and would have predicted only encouraging things for his sons, except God put the words in his mouth. And so Jacob told the truth, no matter how painful that may have been for some of the brothers.

"I am going to die very soon," Jacob told his sons. "I ask that you bury me in the cave of Machpelah. That's where Abraham and Sarah are buried, and Isaac and Rebekah, and that's where I buried Leah."

When Jacob finished talking, he lay his head on his pillow one last time. Then, in the arms of God and with all of his sons surrounding him, he passed to his rest. It was a peaceful end to what had been an often troubled life. Dark clouds had often shadowed Jacob's path, but his last days were spent in sunlight, and the warmth of heaven lit up his final hours.

Jacob was a good man, but the Bible records both the good and the bad about him. God knew that if we saw Jacob's sins and how he overcame at last, it would be an encouragement to us all. If none of the good men in the Bible made any mistakes, we might feel very discouraged. But as we watch them, though beaten back, recovering the ground they have lost, we can gain strength to carry on. Their lives are also a warning to us. If we repeat their mistakes, we, like them, will have a lot of sadness in our lives.

The Bible has some very special verses that talk about the sunset of a person's life. Here are a few that really fit for Jacob.

"When evening comes, there will be light" (Zechariah 14:7).

"Mark the perfect man, and behold the upright: for the end of that man is peace" (Psalm 37:37, KJV).

155

Although Jacob's life had often been difficult, at the end of his days there was light and peace. And this is a promise for us. Even if things go badly in our lives and we make a lot of mistakes, we can have a good ending too.

CHAPTER 32

Waiting for the Promised Land

After Jacob died, again Joseph's brothers started thinking about what they had done to him. Although Joseph had been very good to them, they were worried now that their father was dead. They probably understood the prophecy to Abraham about how his children would be slaves for a while and wondered if it would happen to them right away. In any case, they sent a message to Joseph asking him to forgive them one more time for selling him as a slave.

It made Joseph sad that they dredged their sin up again. His forgiveness of his brothers was true and deep. He was not holding a grudge, and he was not waiting for the death of his father to take revenge. So he reassured his brothers that he would continue to be good to them, and life went on in the land of Egypt.

Perhaps the years of slavery or in the dungeon had taken a toll on Joseph. Or perhaps it was the lifestyle of the Egyptians, who didn't eat healthfully and had many of the diseases we have today. Whatever the case, the Bible seems to say that Joseph died before some of his older brothers. Even though he was more than 100 years old, he was still quite a bit younger than were Abraham, Isaac, or Jacob when they died.

Before he died, Joseph called his brothers to him. "Do not bury me in the land of Egypt," he said. All these years he had wanted to go home, but he knew God needed him in Egypt. However, that didn't keep him from wanting to be buried in the land of his fathers. On the resurrection day, Joseph wanted to wake up next to Abraham, Sarah, Isaac, Rebekah, and Jacob.

"When God brings our children out of Egypt, take my bones with you to the land of Canaan and bury me there."

Joseph's request was honored. When Jacob died, Joseph and an entire procession had carried his body to the cave of Machpelah in Canaan. But when Joseph died, his body rested in Egypt until the people of Israel finally left that land more than 400 years later.

During all those years that coffin was a promise—and a reminder—that they would not be in Egypt forever. The God of Abraham, Isaac, Jacob, and Joseph had promised to bring them back out of Egypt. He would fulfill His word, and when He did, they would take the remains of Joseph with them.

The story of Joseph is one of the most beautiful stories in the Bible. It is also the favorite of many people. Perhaps this is because Joseph, who had so many ups and downs in his life, stayed true to God through it all. When we go through hard times or when people are mean to us, the life of Joseph can be an encouragement that God is still by our side. He will watch out for us, just as He did for Joseph.

We can also learn some interesting things about Jesus by studying the life of Joseph. Joseph is what we call a "type" of Christ. That means that in certain ways, Joseph's life was a mirror of the life of Jesus.

Joseph hailed from the Promised Land, the beautiful land of Canaan. Jesus came from the true Promised Land, the beautiful city of heaven.

Joseph was the beloved son of his father, Jacob. Jesus was the beloved son of His Father, God.

Joseph's father sent him to check on his erring brothers. God sent Jesus to check on His erring children.

Joseph's brothers hated him and treated him cruelly. Jesus received the same type of treatment.

Joseph was sold as a slave for 30 pieces of silver. Jesus was sold to the priests for 30 pieces of silver.

Joseph was falsely accused by Potiphar's wife. Jesus was falsely accused by Satan and the Jews. Joseph went into prison. Jesus went into the prison of death.

Joseph saved his family—and the whole land of Egypt—from the terrible plague of a famine. He did this by storing up lots of food for years and then supplying it to the people when they were very hungry.

Jesus is the Savior of the world. He wants to save you—and many others—from the terrible plague of sin. His great storehouse—the Bible—is packed with spiritual food. Jesus knew that in the last days there would be a famine in the land. People would be hungry to hear the Word of God.

There is life in the Word of God. It is food to the soul and God wants you to hear that Word. Reading your Bible—and the books that point to it—is a great way to learn more about God. Studying and thinking about the life of Bible characters such as Abraham, Sarah, Isaac, Jacob, and Joseph can help you grow close to Jesus. Then when He comes in the clouds, very soon, you can be ready to meet Him.

Joseph died in faith—looking forward to when his family would go to the Promised Land. You may not die, for things are wrapping up very quickly. But you, like Joseph, can look for a better land. Why not give your heart to Jesus today—so you can be ready when He comes in the clouds of heaven.